MW01672368

2013
ROMAN REPLIES
&
CLSA ADVISORY OPINIONS

SR. SHARON A. EUART, RSM, JCD
EDITOR, ROMAN REPLIES

REV. MSGR. JOHN A. ALESANDRO, JCD, JD
REV. MSGR. THOMAS J. GREEN, JCD
EDITORS, ADVISORY OPINIONS

Canon Law Society of America

© Copyright 2013 by the Canon Law Society of America

ISBN 1-932208-36-4
ISSN 1543-4230
SAN 237-6296

The Canon Law Society of America's programs and publications are designed solely to help canonists maintain their professional competence. In dealing with specific canonical matters, the canonist using Canon Law Society of America (CLSA) publications or orally conveyed information should also research original sources of authority.

The views and opinions expressed in this publication are those of the individual authors and do not represent the views of the CLSA, its Board of Governors, staff or members. The CLSA does not endorse the views or opinions expressed by the individual authors. The publisher and authors specifically disclaim any liability, loss or risk, personal or otherwise, which is incurred as consequence, directly or indirectly, of the use, reliance, or application of any of the contents of this publication.

Unless otherwise noted, all canons quoted are from the *Code of Canon Law, Latin-English Edition* (Washington, DC: Canon Law Society of America, 2012) and the *Code of Canons of the Eastern Churches, Latin-English Edition* (Washington, DC: Canon Law Society of America, 2002).

Printed in the United States of America.

Canon Law Society of America
Office of the Executive Coordinator
The Hecker Center, Suite 111
3025 Fourth Street, NE
Washington, DC 20017-1102

Table Of Contents

ADVISORY OPINIONS 2013

FOREWORD

The Canon Law Society of America (CLSA) publishes annually *Roman Replies and CLSA Advisory Opinions* for canonists and those seeking a clearer understanding of the *praxis legis* of the Catholic Church. The combination of these two services, begun in 1984, continues to serve as useful resources for those involved in the application of canonical discipline.

The compilation of materials for *Roman Replies 2013* was guided by Sister Sharon A. Euart, RSM, CLSA Executive Coordinator. The collection of entries in this issue, when viewed in conjunction with previous volumes, assists the reader both in understanding recent developments in the law and in identifying current trends in the praxis of the Roman Curia.

The selection and assembly of opinions for *CLSA Advisory Opinions 2013* was provided by the CLSA Publications Advisory Board, chaired by Monsignor John A. Alesandro. The topics addressed in the opinions reflect a variety of canonical issues and demonstrate the scope of canonical expertise and reflection by members of the Society. Editorial assistance was provided by Mary G. DeBroeck, Administrative Assistant, Office of the Executive Coordinator.

Roman Replies and CLSA Advisory Opinions that are out-of-print are available electronically on the CLSA website (www.clsa.org). As an additional resource, the CLSA Advisory Opinion Online Index includes all published opinions, grouped by canon number on the CLSA website.

The CLSA provides this series as a professional resource. Care should be taken in considering the relative weight of the materials found in this publication. The principles for canonical interpretation (*CIC* cc. 16-19 and *CCEO* cc. 1498-1501) serve as guides in considering the contents of this volume.

Sister Sharon A. Euart, RSM, JCD
Executive Coordinator

Roman Replies

Introductory Note

The following is the editorial policy of Roman Replies. The policy, as well as the source of these materials, was first described in the 1984 edition and, with some modifications, has been in effect since that time.

Each year members of the Canon Law Society of America are invited to submit recent replies from the various dicasteries of the Holy See which might be of interest to the Society's members and the wider church. Judicial vicars, chancellors, vicars general, major superiors of institutes of consecrated life and societies of apostolic life in the United States, and professors of canon law are encouraged and asked to submit material for this important publication.

Contributions from members of the Society resident in other countries or members of other canon law societies are always most welcome. All contributors receive a complimentary copy of the volume.

Certain editorial principles determine the selection of documents for this publication. First, in general, entries which have already appeared in various canonical journals would not normally be repeated here. An exception is the publication of an official English translation of documents which already has been published in an unofficial translation. Second, documents which merely restate something published earlier with no added nuances or changes are not normally included. Third, documents that concern a matter not yet resolved by the Roman dicasteries are held for future publication in the hope that the entire matter may be fully reported when the question or controversy has been resolved. Finally, all details of names and places are changed to protect confidentiality, unless otherwise specified by the submitting individual.

A special note of thanks to all those who have submitted texts, helped with translations and who otherwise contributed to this 2013 edition. It is our hope that this volume continues to be a service to all who work in the ministry of justice in the Church.

Contributions may be sent to:

Canon Law Society of America
Office of the Executive Coordinator
3025 Fourth Street, NE
The Hecker Center, Suite 111
Washington, DC 20017-1102

Canons 50-51, 120-123, 127 §2, 515 §2 and 1222 §2

Procedural Guidelines for the Modification of Parishes and Closure of Parish Churches

To assist Diocesan Bishops in the procedures to modify a parish, close a church, or relegate a parish church to profane use, the Congregation for the Clergy issued "Procedural Guidelines" to address the questions that have arisen in recent years. Below are the Prefect's letter to Diocesan Bishops and the Procedural Guidelines.

CONGREGATION FOR THE CLERGY
Vatican City, 30 April 2013
Prot. No. 20131348

TO THE EMINENT, MOST EXCELLENT,
AND REVEREND ORDINARIES AT THEIR SEES

Your Eminence, Your Excellency,

The Congregation for the Clergy is aware of the significant care and pastoral solicitude with which Bishops have approached the modification of parishes (cf. can. 515 §2) and the relegation to profane use or even the simple closure of churches (cf. can. 1222 §2). Despite their best efforts, however, various difficulties concerning these questions have arisen in recent years, both for Bishops and for the faithful. In an effort to provide helpful guidance and thereby to prevent many of the difficulties heretofore experienced, this Dicastery presents the attached descriptions of the canonical procedures and jurisprudence concerning the above-mentioned processes.

Before proceeding to more specific information, some preliminary observations will prove helpful. First, it is necessary to distinguish clearly between three separate and distinct canonical processes: (1) the modification of parishes, (2) the relegation to profane use and/or the permanent closure of churches, and (3) the alienation of current or former sacred edifices. Each process has its own procedures, and each must be followed carefully and correctly. It should be noted that no process at all is required to close a church temporarily, such as for repairs. The same is true for restricting its use by such things as eliminating the celebration of Sunday Mass, provided that the church remain open for the access of the faithful (cf. can. 1214).

Secondly, when treating the modification of parishes and the relegation or closure of churches, there is a need for much greater clarity in distinguishing the juridic person of a diocese from the juridic person of a parish. Nowhere is this more apparent than in questions concerning the ownership of churches, and who is responsible for their upkeep. Likewise, it should be noted that some commonly-used terms in these processes, e.g., "suppression", have both a broad non-technical meaning as well as a precise canonical meaning. In order to avoid unnecessary confusion, it is best in canonical documents to avoid the non-technical use of such terms.

In determining whether or not the required just cause is present in the case of a proposed parish modification (cf. can. 515 §2) or the required grave cause in the case of church closure and relegation (cf. can. 1222 §2), each case must be considered separately. Although the Bishop may take into consideration the needs of surrounding parishes or even that of the diocese as a whole, he must always motivate his decree with a cause that is specific, i.e., *ad rem*, to the individual parish or church under consideration.

Lastly, each administrative decision must be enacted by a separate written decree, issued and lawfully communicated at the time that the decision is given. Because the just cause for a parish modification and the grave cause for the relegation or closure of a church are not the same, decisions regarding these processes should be issued in separate decrees.

In a spirit of fraternal collaboration, keeping in mind the responsibilities incumbent upon every Diocesan Bishop, and desiring always the good of the Church, I take this opportunity to renew my sentiments of esteem and collegial affection, and I remain

Sincerely yours in Christ,

(Signed)
Mauro Cardinal Piacenza
Prefect

(Signed)
Celso Morga Iruzubieta
Titular Archbishop of Alba marittima
Secretary

PROCEDURAL GUIDELINES FOR THE MODIFICATION OF PARISHES, THE CLOSURE OR RELEGATION OF CHURCHES TO PROFANE BUT NOT SORDID USE, AND THE ALIENATION OF THE SAME

1. *Modification of parishes*

The relevant canons are chiefly can. 515, and also cann. 50, 51, 120, 121, 122, 123, 127, and 166.

A parish is a community of the faithful which, being a juridic person *ipso iure*, is perpetual by its nature (cf. can. 120 §1, and can. 515 §§1, 3). It cannot be extinguished or even notably altered without just cause.

There are four possible types of parish modifications. They are known by a variety of terms, sometimes interchangeably, in the various languages, leading to imprecision in decrees and other canonical documents. Such documents, however, cannot allow for imprecision. As an example, all four of these types of modifications are occasionally referred to as "suppressions", but it is clearly best to limit the use of that term in canonical documents to the fourth type, so as to avoid confusion. Likewise, the type of extinctive union intended should be clearly indicated in a decree. The four types of modifications are:

i. extinctive union: (sometimes known as merger)

A and B unite to form C, only C remains (cf. can. 121)

ii. extinctive union: (sometimes also known as merger, or as amalgamation)

A is subsumed into B, only B remains (by analogy to can. 121)

iii. total division:

A is divided into B and C, only B and C remain (cf. can. 122)

iv. suppression:

A is extinguished ... nothing remains (cf. can. 123)

Since parishes are communities of the faithful, territorial parishes as a general rule can only be united or divided (cf. cann. 121and 122). Although sometimes personal parishes are truly suppressed (cf. can. 123), they are ordinarily united or divided, either in connection to another personal parish or even to a territorial parish.

The authority competent to erect, suppress, or notably alter parishes is the diocesan Bishop or those equivalent to him in law (cf. cann. 381§2, 368, and 515 §2). He is competent to judge the existence of the required just cause, but his judgment must conform to ecclesiastical jurisprudence.

According to this jurisprudence, the principal motivation for modifying a parish is a concern for souls (*Christus Dominus* no. 32) and this modification should be undertaken when the good of the faithful requires it (*Apostolorum Successores*, no. 214, which is listed as no. 215 in the Italian text).

Jurisprudence indicates that an extinctive union or suppression should be the last choice when dealing with various problems affecting parochial life, insofar as other possible remedies should have been at least considered beforehand and ruled out.

Furthermore, jurisprudence acknowledges that the diocesan Bishop can and sometimes should consider the good of the whole diocese in making his decision. Nonetheless, the reason(s) for modifying a particular parish must be relevant to that individual parish, i.e., the cause must be *ad rem*. Generalized or diocesan motivations alone cannot justify the modification of a specific parish.

Before rendering his decision, the Bishop must seek out the necessary information and, insofar as possible, hear those whose rights could be injured (cf. can. 50). Before consulting the members of the Presbyteral Council, which is required for validity, he must first provide them with all relevant information, lawfully convoke the Council (cf. cann. 127 and 166), and then he himself must consult the members regarding each individual parish modification which has been proposed. The consultation must be genuine, and should consider relevant arguments both for and against the proposed modifications.

Any decree modifying a parish must be issued in writing at the time that the decision is given and then lawfully communicated without delay. The period of time during which hierarchical recourse may be presented begins with the lawful notification of the decree (cf. can. 1734 §2). In addition, the decree must mention at least in summary form the just cause(s) for the decision (cf. can. 51).

The decree must clearly define the criteria for membership in all parishes affected by the modification.

The decree must likewise provide for the disposition of temporal goods in accord with law, and must respect the intentions of donors (cf. cann. 121, 122, and 123). Jurisprudence has clearly established that when parishes are modified, the temporal goods are to follow the people.

2. *Closure of churches / Relegation of churches to profane but not sordid use*

The relevant canons are chiefly cann. 1214 and 1222, and also cann. 50, 51, 127, and 166.

Regardless of which juridic person owns a sacred edifice, or of the extent to which it is open, or of the popular designation by which it is called, e.g. a "mission", "chapel of devotion", "oratory", or "worship site", the law understands a church to be any sacred edifice designated for divine worship to which the faithful have the right of entry for the exercise of divine worship, especially public worship (cf. can. 1214).

There is a clear disposition both in law and in tradition that a sacred edifice which has been given over perpetually for divine worship should retain that sacred character if at all possible, and only a grave reason to the contrary is sufficient to justify relegating a church to profane but not sordid use (cf. can. 1222 §2). Even more so, altars do not lose their dedication or blessing when the church does, and can never be turned over to profane use for any reason (cf. cann. 1212 and 1238).

It is well established in ecclesiastical jurisprudence that merely to close a church permanently, even without any intention to turn it over to profane use, is juridically equivalent to relegating it to profane use. Consequently, one cannot lawfully permanently close a church without first employing the provisions of can. 1222 §2, with the corollary that in the absence of applying the provisions of can. 1222 §2, the church is to remain open.

The authority competent to relegate a church to profane but not sordid use according to the norm of can. 1222 §2 is the diocesan Bishop or those equivalent to him in law (cf. cann. 381 §2, 368, and 515 §2). He is competent to judge the existence of the required grave cause, but his judgment must conform to ecclesiastical jurisprudence.

To assess the gravity of a cause, each case must be considered individually, weighing the whole context of the situation. At times, the gravity of a cause will arise only from a combination of just causes, each insufficient in itself, but which together manifest the seriousness of the situation.

When considering questions of finances, the relevant financial need is that of the juridic person which owns the church and is therefore responsible for it.

Furthermore, it must be demonstrated that other reasonable sources of funding or assistance have been considered and found lacking or inadequate.

Because churches can remain sacred edifices even though they are only occasionally or even rarely used, jurisprudence has established that the following reasons in themselves do not constitute grave cause:

i. a general plan of the diocese to reduce the number of churches

ii. the church is no longer needed

iii. the parish has been suppressed

iv. the number of parishioners has decreased

v. closure will not harm the good of souls

vi. a desire to promote the unity of the parish

vii. some potential future cause that has not actually happened yet

i) Before rendering his decision, the Bishop must seek out the necessary proofs and, insofar as possible, hear those whose rights could be injured (cf. can. 50). In addition, before consulting the members of the Presbyteral Council, which is required for validity, he must first provide them with all relevant information, lawfully convoke the Council (cf. cann. 127 and 166), and then he himself must consult the members regarding each individual relegation which has been proposed. The consultation must be genuine, and should consider relevant arguments both for and against the proposed relegation. He must also obtain the consent of those who claim legitimate rights in the edifice (cf. cann. 1222 §2 and 127) and verify that the good of souls will suffer no harm (cf. can 1222 §2).

j) The Bishop must give his decision by means of a written decree issued in writing at the time when the decision is given and then lawfully communicated without delay. The period of time during which hierarchical recourse may be presented begins with the lawful notification of the decree (cf. can. 1734 §2). In addition, the decree must mention at least in summary form the grave cause(s) for the decision (cf. can. 51).

3. *Alienation of churches*

The relevant canons are chiefly cann. 1291-1298, and also cann. 50, 51, 127, and 166.

The canons on alienation apply not only to the actual sale of an edifice, but also to other transactions which could harm the stable patrimony of the juridic person which owns it (cf. can. 1295).

If after it is alienated, a church will remain in use as a Catholic place for divine worship to which the faithful have a continued right of access, e.g., by sale to a different Ritual Church *sui iuris*, it should not be relegated to profane use prior to the alienation. In all other situations, however, it must be relegated to profane but not sordid use prior to being alienated.

If it becomes necessary to alienate the edifice, various options, listed in decreasing order of preference are:

i. for continued use as a place of Catholic worship (non-relegated)

ii. for use as a place for the exercise of other Catholic apostolates or ministries

iii. for profane but not sordid use in keeping with the dignity of the edifice as a former church

iv. demolition of the edifice, recovering the land

Under no circumstances can the edifice be alienated for use inconsistent with its inherent dignity as a former church. Contractual agreements are to be put in place to safeguard this point in civil law as well as canonically.

Furthermore, the competent authority must assure that there is no reasonable possibility of scandal or loss of the faithful which will result from the proposed alienation.

Prior to alienation, all sacred objects, relics, sacred furnishings, stained-glass windows, bells, confessionals, altars, etc. are to be removed for use in other sacred edifices or to be stored in ecclesiastical custody. Because altars can never be turned over to profane use, if they cannot be removed, they must be destroyed (cf. cann. 1212 and 1238).

Regarding the procedures for alienation:

i. When the value of the edifice lies beneath the minimum amount established by the Episcopal Conference, the competent authority is the pastor or that defined by the statutes, unless particular law determines otherwise. That authority must have at least a just cause to alienate the edifice.

ii. When the value of the edifice lies between minimum and maximum amounts, the competent authority must have a just cause for alienation, together with written appraisal by experts (cf. can. 1293). For juridic persons which are not subject to the Bishop, the competent authority is identified by the statues. In all other cases, it is the diocesan Bishop, who must also have the consent of the diocesan Finance Council, the consent of the College of Consultors, and the consent of interested parties (cf. cann. 1292 §1, 127, and 166).

iii. When value of the edifice exceeds the maximum amount established by the Episcopal Conference, or if the edifice was given by vow, or is precious for artistic or historical reasons, then the competent authority, either that identified by the statues or the diocesan Bishop, must also have the consent of the Holy See (cf. can. 1292 §2).

Canons 51, 127 §2, 515 §2, 1222 §2, 1292 §2, and 1734

Closing a Church and Relegation of the Church to Profane but not Sordid Use

A Diocesan Bishop, having completed a pastoral planning process, received a request from the pastor of a parish recommedning that one of the remaining churches in the parish be closed. The Diocesan Bishop requested the relegation of the Church to profane but not sordid use and obtained the necessary approvals in accord with canons 1222 §2 and 127 §2. Several "recurrents" requested reconsideration of the decision by the Diocesan Bishop. After the Bishop indicated that he would not revoke or change the decree, the recurrents sought hierarchical recourse from the Congregation for the Clergy in accord with canon 1737. Below is the Congregation's response.

CONGREGATION FOR THE CLERGY
Vatican City, ______ 2012
Prot. N. ______

Your Excellency,

This Congregation has received and thanks Your Excellency for your letter of ______ last, concerning the relegation of the church of X to profane but not sordid use.

The Dicastery has now issued a canonical response to this recourse, which is enclosed for the timely information of Your Excellency, together with a copy of the letters of transmission both to the recurrents and the diocesan procurator-advocate.

In keeping with the dignity which inherently belongs to buildings once used as churches, the relegated church is not to be alienated to any purchaser who is likely to use it for non-Christian worship or for any other purpose contrary to the doctrinal or moral teaching of the Church. Your Excellency is courteously reminded that, in certain circumstances (cf. 1292 §2), the permission of this Congregation is required before alienation of the property may take place.

In order to avoid the danger of scandal or of profanation of sacred objects, moveable altars and sacred objects are to be transferred to another Catholic church, or otherwise entrusted to ecclesiastical care. With regard to fixed altars and other fixed sacred objects, the relics deposited in or below any altar are to be removed and entrusted to ecclesiastical care, after which such altars and any other fixed sacred objects are to be removed for future use in another Catholic church, if possible, or otherwise destroyed (cf. cann. 1238, 1212).

I avail myself of this opportunity to renew my sentiments of esteem and with ever best wish, I remain,

Sincerely yours in Christ,

(Signed)
+ Celso Morga Iruzubieta
Titular Archbishop of Alba Maritima
[Enclosures]

Prot. N. ______

DECREE

1. Whereas, by a decree of July 24, 1992, the then Bishop of ______, the Most Reverend ______, merged four parishes in ______, establishing a new territorial parish of ______ (can 515 §2), and relegated two churches to profane but not sordid use (can. 1222 §2), retaining the churches of Y and X and establishes the church of Y as the center of pastoral activity of the parish, and the location of the parish school and rectory;

2. Whereas, following a pastoral planning process in 2007-2009, it was recommended that one of the remaining churches in the parish of ______ should be closed, and one should remain open as the parish church;

3. Whereas on May 14, 2011 the pastor of the parish of ______ presented a petition to the Bishop of ______, the Most Reverend ______ (hereinafter called "the Ordinary"), requesting the relegation of the church X to profane but not sordid use, such petition being co-signed by members of the Parish Finance Council and Parish Pastoral Council, with three members indicating their dissent;

4. Whereas on May 24, 2011 the Ordinary consulted the Presbyteral Council on the possible reduction of the Church X to profane but not sordid use, in accordance with cann. 1222 §2 and 127 §1;

5. Whereas on July 1, 2011 the Ordinary issued a decree relegating the church X to profane but not sordid use, and in that decree set forth his motives for its issue in accordance with can. 51, and notified its contents to the members of the parish on July 16, 2011.

6. Whereas on July 25, 2011 ______, ______, ______, ______, ______, and ______ (hereinafter called "the recurrents") wrote to the Ordinary requesting the reconsideration and reversal of his decree, in accordance with can. 1734;

7. Whereas on August 12, 2011 the Ordinary wrote to the recurrents indicating that he would not revoke or amend his decree, and giving his reasons for that decision;

8. Whereas on August 29, 2011 the recurrents sent their request for hierarchical recourse to the Congregation for the Clergy in accordance with can. 1737, this recourse being considered to have been legitimately placed within the peremptory time limits;

9. Whereas on November 21, 2011 in response to the inquiry of this Dicastery into the matter, the Ordinary submitted his *votum* and the acts of the cause;

10. Whereas on July 5, 2012 the recurrents submitted further observations to this Congregation, taking issue with the motives contained in the decree of July 1, 2011, and challenging the assertions of the Ordinary as to the financial state of the parish;

11. Whereas on July 16, 2012 the Ordinary submitted a further *votum* and further acts to this Dicastery, including a detailed analysis of the financial state of the parish, and presenting a more thorough explanation of the motives for his decision: since the establishment of the parish of ______, all parish and school activity has been based at the church Y, owing largely to the state of the parochial buildings at the church X; the location of the church Y is more convenient for the large majority of the diminished number of parishioners, the neighborhood in which the church X is situated is considered unsafe and many local, commercial and residential buildings having been abandoned; only one weekly Mass was celebrated in the church X and, owing to the shortage of clergy, this situation would not improve; the lack of parish funds to maintain two churches, coupled with the inability to make the capital investment required to demolish the parochial buildings adjacent to the church X and to make necessary repairs and improvements to the church itself, which would ultimately lead to it falling into ruin.

12. Whereas an hierarchical recourse is, by its nature, a documentary process which proceeds on the basis of examination of authentic documents provided by interested parties at the request of this Congregation; thus having provided by interested parties at the request of this Congregation; thus having provided ample opportunity for all interested parties to respond and having carefully examined the documents submitted by both the Ordinary and the recurrents, this Dicastery judges as complete the documentation in its possession and proceeds therefore to its decision *per cartas*;

13. As concerns the procedure required by can. 1222 §2, the acts show that, having received the formal petition of the parish priest of May 14, 2011 to relegate the church X to profane but not sordid use, the Ordinary consulted the Presbyteral Council on May 24, 2011. The minutes of the meeting show that the members unanimously favoured the relegation of the church to profane but not sordid use. The only person revealed in the acts who could lawfully claim rights over the church within the meaning of can. 1222 §2 is the parish priest, whose consent is manifested in his letter to the Ordinary and the accompanying petition of May 14, 2011. The acts further show that the Ordinary issued a motivated decree on July 1, 2011. This Congregation considers that the procedure followed is both valid and lawful.

14. As concerns the decision taken, can. 1222 §2 imposes a duty on the Ordinary to show a grave reason that a church should no longer be used for divine worship. The motivating causes contained in the decree of July 1, 2011 are the enhancement of the liturgical, pastoral and spiritual unity of the parish, the lack of financial resources to maintain the church X, the lack of architectural, historical or artistic significance to the building and the continuing maintenance diminishing the care of souls. Although some of the reasons expressed do not constitute a grave cause in themselves, this Dicastery finds that there are sufficient reasons provided by the Ordinary both within his decree and his statements to this Congregation, as summarized in paragraph 11 hereof, which, when taken together, are indeed grave. This Dicastery further finds that the Ordinary has taken suitable steps to ensure that the good of souls will not be harmed by the relegation of the church X, to profane but not sordid use.

Therefore:

> This Congregation hereby decrees that this petition for hierarchical recourse as presented, with regard to the decree of relegation of the church X in the Diocese of ______ to profane but not sor-

did use does not have a canonical basis either in law or in fact and is rejected both *in procedendo* and *in decernendo*.

Recourse against this Decree may be made before the Supreme Tribunal of the Apostolic Signatura within the peremptory time limit established by the Apostolic Letter *Motu Proprio, Antiqua Ordinatione* 34 §1.

Given at the Seat of the Congregation for the Clergy,

______, 2012

(Signed) Mauro Cardinal Piacenza *Prefect*	(Signed) Celso Morga Iruzubieta *Titular Archbishop of Alba Maritima* *Secretary*

Canons 134, 601, 1319, and 1734-1737

Imposition of a Precept of Obedience by the Superior Gereral of a Women's Religious Institute on a Member

A major superior of a pontifical women's religious institute imposed a penal precept on a member. The member appealed the decision to the Congregation for Institutes of Consecrated Life and Societies of Apostolic Life. The superior's decision was not upheld since the power of governance (cc. 129 §1 and 134 §1) can be exercised only by those in Sacred Orders. The precept was revoked. The superior then imposed an obedience on the same member in virtue of the vow of obedience. The member sought recourse from CICLSAL against the decision. Below is the Congregation's response.

CONGREGATION FOR INSTITUTES OF CONSECRATED LIFE AND SOCIETIES OF APOSTOLIC LIFE

Vatican City, ______, 2012
Prot. N. ______

Dear Sr. ______,

Please find enclosed, for your information, a copy of the Decree (dated 2 July 2012) which has been issued by this Dicastery, concerning the recourse presented by Sr. ______ against the penal precept you imposed on 28 November, 2011.

Yours sincerely in Christ,

(Signed)
Sr. Nicoletta V. Spezzati, A.S.C.
Undersecretary

PART I

Prot. N. ______

DECREE

I. The Facts

1. The Superior General of the Congregation of ______, in her letter of 28 November, 2011 imposed a penal precept on Sr. ______, in accordance with can. 1319.

Sr. ______ was notified of this decision on the day it was issued, but only on 14 December 2011 did she have the possibility of obtaining the help of a legal advisor, which enabled her, on that same date, to present her request to the Superior General for the revocation of this precept, in accordance with can. 1734 §1.

2. The Superior General, in her letter of 14 January 2012, gave a negative reply to this request for revocation (can. 1735). In response, Sr. ______ presented administrative hierarchical recourse, in accordance with can. 1737 §1, to this Dicastery in her letter of 17 January 2012, which was within the time limit established in can. 1737 §2.

II. In Law and in Fact

3. Can. 1734 §2 states that the request for revocation *must be made within the peremptory time-limit of ten canonical days from the time the decree was lawfully notified.*

Because the precept was notified on 28 November 2011, Sr. ______ should have presented her request for revocation to the Superior General by 8 December, 2011.

However, although she presented the petition on 14 December 2011, which was six days after the limit stated in can. 1734 §2, it must be acknowledged that Sr. ______ had clearly demonstrated her intention to consult a priest and a religious sister, the chancellor of the Diocese of ______, on the very day she was notified, that is the 28 November, 2011 and during the days immediately following, in order to obtain legal assistance in the recourse that she wanted to present.

Nevertheless, Sr. ______ did not succeed in obtaining this legal advice until 14 December 2011. Thus it was only on this date that she was able to present her request to the Superior General for revocation of the precept which had been issued on 28 November 2011.

4. Thus the reasons why Sr. ______ did not present her request for revocation by 8 December 2011 were not exclusively related to her intention, but to her difficulty in obtaining legal advice which made it impossible for her to do so. Because this advice was obtained only a few days after the expiry of the time limit given in can. 1737 §2, at which time she immediately presented her petition for revocation, this Dicastery has decided that her petition should be considered legitimately presented within the canonical time limit.

5. Canon 1319 §1 states that *to the extent to which a legislator can impose precepts by virtue of the power of governance in the external forum, to that extent can he also by precept threaten a determined penalty* ... Therefore, a penal precept can only be imposed by authorities in Sacred Orders (can. 129 §1) who are also considered to be Ordinaries in the terms of can. 134 §1.

Can. 134 §1, however, does not attribute such a type of power to any Major Superior of a religious Institute of women, that is, not a clerical Institute, of pontifical or of diocesan right.

As a consequence, since the precept of 28 November 2011 was issued in accordance with can. 1319 ("in accord with canon 1319, I hereby issue to you this penal precept") and hence the intention to attribute to it the nature of a penal precept cannot be in doubt; considering also that the precept in question has been issued by the Superior General of the Institute to which Sr. ______ belongs, which is an authority without the power of jurisdiction in the sense given in can. 129 §1 and 134 §1, it can be deduced with certainty that the precept in question was issued by an authority which was not competent to do so.

6. Therefore, this Congregation for Institutes of Consecrated Life and Societies of Apostolic Life, having heard the opinion of the *Congresso* of 15 June 2012, with this present decree accepts the recourse presented by Sr. ______ in her letter of 17 January 2012. At the same time it also revokes the precept concerning Sr. ______, issued on 28 November, 2011 by the Superior General of the Congregation ______.

7. In addition to the above, it is to be understood that acceptance of this recourse does not intend in any way to express a judgment about the merits of the reasons for which the Superior General emitted this precept of 28 November 2011 and for which she might consider it appropriate to adopt disciplinary measures of a different nature from the precept of 28 November 2011.

All things to the contrary notwithstanding

Given at Vatican City, 2 July 2012

(Signed)
+ Joseph W. Tobin, C.Ss.R.
Archbishop Secretary

(Signed)
Sr. Nicoletta V. Spezzati, A.S.C.
Undersecretary

PART II

Prot. N. _______

DECREE

THE MATTER AT HAND

1. In virtue of the vow of obedience, with a letter dated 24 August 2012, the Superior General of the Congregation of _______, imposed an obedience upon Sr. _______, a perpetually professed Sister in a Religious Institute of Pontifical Right. The obedience contained the following directives upon Sr. _______:

- to cease your disruptive behavior during community meetings.
- to cease speaking when so commanded by the chair of the community meeting.
- to cease public opposition to decisions of the Leadership of the community unless recognized to speak during a community meeting. If you are so recognized, you are to state your position on the matter and not continuously argue against the decision of the Leadership.
- to cease public opposition to decisions of the community unless recognized to speak during a community meeting. If you are to state your position on the matter and not continuously argue against the decision of the community.
- to speak respectfully regarding the opinions and positions of others.
- to cease making efforts covertly to influence the opinions of the sisters in order to gain support for your own ideas.
- to refrain from any involvement in or attempts to interfere with processes of election within the community.

2. Sr. _______, considering the above directives of the precept of obedience to be a violation of the rights conferred upon her by membership in the institute, with a letter dated August 28, 2012, or within the time limit mentioned in canon 1734 §2, presented a request for the revocation of the obedience in question to the Superior General, the author of the obedience.

3. In response, the Major Superior, with a letter dated September 17, 2012, rejected the request for the revocation presented by Sr. _______. Consequently, the religious in question, with a letter dated September 19, 2012, or within the time limit mentioned in canons 1735 and 1737 §2, in accordance with the provisions of canon 1737 §1, presented an administrative hierarchical recourse to this Congregation for Institutes of Consecrated Life and Societies of Apostolic Life. Since the Congregation of _______ is a Religious Institute of Pontifical Right and given the fact that the above-mentioned letter of the Superior General to Sr. _______, dated 28 August 2012, must be considered, even if not in format, at least in substance, a decree; in accord with article n. 107 of the Apostolic Constitution *Pastor Bonus*, the Congregation for Institutes of Consecrated Life and Societies of Apostolic Life is the competent entity to receive and to make a decision regarding the matter. This Decree is written as a response to the recourse presented.

THE LAW

4. Canon 601 states: The evangelical counsel of obedience, undertaken in the spirit of faith and love in the following of Christ, who was obedient even unto death, obliges submission of one's will to lawful Superiors, who act in the place of God when they give commands that are in accordance with each institute's own constitutions. Therefore, every religious has the duty to follow orders received from a competent Superior, both local and Major, especially if given in a serious matter and/or as a precept imposed in virtue of the vow of obedience, even if they require a special effort of the will. At the same time, those provisions should be given in accordance with the Constitutions of the Institute and the Universal Law of the Church, or at least should not be in conflict with those provisions. Canon 1737 §1 gives the right of recourse to anyone who, for any reason, believes that his/her rights have been violated. A nun may present a recourse against a decree only if it directly and/or indirectly violates rights recognized and/or particularly assigned by proper and/or universal law.

IN FACT

5. Sr. _______, in her letter of 19 September 2012, said she believe her rights as a perpetually professed religious of the Congregation of _______ had been violated, since the provisions of the General Superior, in her letter of August 25, 2012, would have prevented her from fully participating in congregational meetings in accord with rights and obligations arising from profession as indicated in their Constitutions, or the rights and duties stipulated in Articles nn. 63, 65 and 66 of the Constitutions. More specifically, Article n. 63 gives professed religious of the institute the right to active and passive voice according to the Constitutions and shared responsibility for the proper conduct of life, mission and apostolate of the Institute. Article n. 63 states: *A sister in perpetual vows has active and passive voice in the congregation according to the Constitution. With the other perpetually professed members of the congregation she is responsible for the life, mission and ministry of the congregation.* Article n. 65 foresees that the General Government of the Institute must seek above all the promotion of fraternal communion between religious and the pursuit of the common good: *the purpose of the government of the congregation is to embody and promote loving communion of persons and to promote the attainment of communal goals. The success of the government of the congregation depends upon the willingness of the sisters to participate in determining, achieving and evaluating goals in an atmosphere of open and free communication.* Finally, Article n. 66 points out that, in the Institute, fraternal communion is founded on dialogue and participation in religious discernment to make decisions and, likewise, in the sharing of responsibilities. In fact, said art. n. 66 states: *in the congregation, emphasis is placed on dialogue and participation so that the sisters are involved in the process of making decisions and they share the responsibility and accountability for them.*

6. Taking into account the above cited articles, the reasons given by Sr. _______ for her recourse are not adequately substantiated. In fact, the directives imposed by the Superior General with the August 24, 2012 precept of obedience do not deprive Sr. _______ of active and/or passive voice as indicated in art. n. 63, nor do they prohibit the possibility of the religious participating in discussions and discernment regarding decisions for the good of the Institute and/or the individual religious, nor do they prohibit her from cooperating in the implementation of initiatives/

activities decided upon for the proper conduct of the life, mission and apostolate of the Institute (arts. nos. 63, 66), nor of offering a contribution for the realization of fraternal communion (art. no. 65). Rather, the precept against which Sr. _______ filed a recourse only regards the manner of participating in the various activities of the common life of the Institute, demanding a more respectful behavior, understanding and willingness to accept the opinions of others and the decisions taken by the Superiors and the community, especially when they are contrary to or just different from her beliefs.

In summary, this Dicastery has not found, in the reasons presented in the present recourse, nor in the recourse in question, elements in the directives given in virtue of the vow of obedience by the Superior General, in a letter dated August 24, 2012, which are directly or indirectly contrary to the regulations of the Institute or of the Universal Church or which have violated the rights of the religious who has presented the recourse.

Therefore, having carefully evaluated the documents in its possession for the legality of the procedure followed and having affirmed that the applicant was granted the right to defend herself, after consultation in a *Congresso* held on April 5, 2013, this Congregation for Institutes of Consecrated Life and Societies of Apostolic Life, in view of the reasons aforementioned, with the present Decree, in accordance with canon 1739, rejects the recourse presented and thereby confirms the directives given to Sr. _______ by the General Superior of the Congregation of _______ in her letter of August 24, 2012.

Notwithstanding any provision to the contrary.

Given at Vatican City, _______, 2013

(Signed)
P. Sebastiano Paciolla, O. Cist
Undersecretary

(Signed)
Waldemar Barcszcz, TOR
Office Head

Canon 290

Dispensation from the Obligations of the Clerical State

The Congregation for the Clergy sent a set of guestions to a Diocesan Bishop in response to a request for questions for petitioners used in instructing cases for dispensation from obligations of the clerical state.

Interrogation of the Petitioner

(All questions must be answered by the Petitioner under oath)

1. Your full name.
2. Exact date and place of birth.
3. Tell of your family background, the family's economic situation, parent's occupation, etc.
4. Were you free and sincere in your decision to remain celibate before your ordination to the diaconate?
5. What was the exact date of your ordination to the priesthood?
6. What studies did you accomplish before entering the Seminary, or during your time in the Minor Seminary? How many years did you study?
7. What studies did you accomplish during your time in the seminary prior to your ordination? Where did you do them? For how many years?
8. Did you accomplish any further studies? Which ones? Where? For how many years?
9. What pastoral work or apostolate did you carry out before your ordination?
10. List all appointments you were given after your ordination.
11. Did you have any difficulty in your early years of Seminary?
12. And during your studies of Philosophy?
13. Did you have any difficulty during your Theology studies or any other time prior to your ordination?

14. Did you have any difficulty after your ordination to the Priesthood? Which were they and how did you deal with them?

15. What made you think of becoming a priest? Describe as clearly as you can your motivation for entering the Seminary.

16. Was your decision free or felt to be free to join the Seminary? Did you feel any pressure from anyone to enter the Seminary?

17. Did you get on well with the formation staff? What would you say about the competence and way of acting of the formation staff and Superiors: a) in the early years of Seminary; b) during the main time of formation in the Seminary; c) during the last years of Seminary.

18. Did you suffer any physical or psychological illness? Did you consult a practitioner or specialist in the field? What was their opinion? Do you have a record? What did they do to solve your problem?

19. Were you responsible for any serious failure to your Christian commitments or obligations prior to ordination?

20. If so, how did you deal with them? Did you discuss it: a) with your Superiors? b) with any other? What was their opinion or advice?

21. When did you decide to leave or no longer continue a celibate life? What was the nature of the dissatisfaction?

22. Did you decide to leave the Priesthood at the same time? What were the circumstances that led up to this decision? What were the reasons behind it?

23. When did you leave your ministry and effectively cease to exercise the Priesthood?

24. Did you have the consent of your Ordinary? What sort of authorization precisely did you have?

25. Where are you living now: with your family or in another circumstance? What is your current occupation? Provide your current address: street, number, city, postcode, etc. In which Diocese is this found?

26. Have you attempted civil marriage? If so, what is the name of the woman? Is she free to marry? Or, are you cohabitating with her without having attempted civil marriage?

27. Do you have any children?

28. What are you requesting now concerning your obligations towards the Priesthood?

29. What are you reasons for requesting this dispensation?

30. Are you certain about your decision? Is your request of dispensation from the obligations of Holy Orders including celibacy considered as something definitive?

31. Have you been informed and are you aware that once you have been dispensed and returned to the lay state you will no longer be able or capable of exercising any priestly office or ministry?

32. Do you wish to change anything, to add, or withdraw anything from the evidence you have given?

(Place, day, month, year)
(Signature of the petitioning priest)
(Signature of the priest Instructor and notary taking the deposition)
(Stamp of the diocesan/provincial seal)

CANON 293

DISPENSATION FOR TRANSITIONAL DEACON WHO WAS LAICIZED AND MARRIED TO BE ADMITTED TO THE PERMANENT DIACONATE

A Diocesan Bishop requested a dispensation for a laicized and married transitional deacon to be readmitted to serve the Church as a permanent deacon. The letter and rescript of the Congregation for Divine Worship and Discipline of the Sacraments follow.

CONGREGATION FOR DIVINE WORSHIP AND DISCIPLINE OF THE SACRAMENTS

Prot. N.____

Your Excellency,

Enclosed with this letter please find the Rescript of dispensation requested on behalf of Dr. ______, a transitional deacon for the Diocese of ______, who has been laicized and was married in 1972, and recently retired from a long and dedicated career working as a layman for the ______, so that he now can be readmitted exceptionally to serve the Church as a permanent deacon incardinated in your Archdiocese.

This Congregation for Divine Worship and the Discipline of Sacraments would ask that, though communicating this dispensation to the aforementioned deacon with all pastoral sensitivity, Your Excellency would impose upon him as a salutary penance, the making of a Thirty-Day retreat.

With every good wish and kind regard,

Devotedly yours in Christ,

(Signed)
+ Antonio Card. Cañizares Llovera
Prefect

His Excellency
The Most Reverend ______
Archbishop of ______, USA

DECREE
UNOFFICIAL ENGLISH TRANSLATION

Prot. N. ______

Most Holy Father,

Mr. ______, formerly a deacon of the Diocese of ______ , dispensed from the obligations flowing from Sacred Orders and dismissed from the clerical state, bowing at the feet of Your Holiness, humbly begs to be enrolled among clerics again and reintegrated in the diaconal ministry since the reasons for which he lost the clerical state are no longer operative.

From an audience with His Holiness ______ 2012

His Holiness Pope Benedict XVI, after hearing a report from the Cardinal Secretary of State in an audience granted him, in view of the circumstances mentioned in the petition and responding favorably to the *votum* of the Ordinary, grants the faculty that has been sought in accord with the norm of canon 293 of the Code of Canon Law.

Anything to the contrary notwithstanding.

Given in Rome at the Congregation for Divine Worship and the Discipline of the Sacraments, ______ 2012.

(Signed)
Antonius Cardinal Cañizares Llovera
Prefect

(Signed)
+ Ioanes Michael Ferrer Grenesche
Sub-Secretary

Prot. N. ______

Beatissime Pater,

Dominus ______, olim diaconus ______ dioecesis, ac iam dispensatus ab obligationibus Sacrae Ordinationi conexis et dimissus e statu clericali, cum desint rationes quibus statum clericalem amissit, ad pedes Sanctitatis Vestrae provolutus, humiliter postulat denuo adscribi inter clericos ac reintegrari in ministerio diaconali.

Ex Audientia SS.mi diei ______ 2012

SS.mus D.N. BENEDICTUS PP. XVI, audita relatione Em.mi Cardinalis Secretarii Status in Audientia Eidem concessa, attentis circumstantiis in supplici libello relatis ac votis Exc.mi Ordinarii ______. Accedens, petitam facultatem concedit, ad normam can. 293 Codicis iuris canonici.

Contrariis quibuslibet minime obstantibus.

Datum Romae ex aedibus Congregationis de Cultu Divino et Disicplina Sacramentorum, ______ 2012.

(Signed)
Antonius Card. Cañizares Llovera
Praefectus

(Signed)
+ Ioanes Michael Ferrer Grenesche
Sub Secretarius

Canons 579, 587 §2 and 595 §1

Erection of a Public Association of the Faithful as a Religious Institute of Diocesan Right

In 199___ a community was erected as a Public Association of the Faithful in accordance with canons 298-320. In 2011, the foundress petitioned the diocesan bishop to erect the community as an Institute of Diocesan Right. In accordance with canon 579, the bishop sought the consent of the Congregation for Institutes of Consecrated Life and Societies of Apostolic Life by sending the required documents. Below are the Congregation's response (English original) and the bishop's decree.

CONGREGATION FOR INSTITUTES OF CONSECRATED LIFE AND SOCIETIES OF APOSTOLIC LIFE
Vatican City, ___2012
Prot. N.____

Your Excellency,

Having carefully examined all the documents presented to this *Congregation for Institutes of Consecrated Life and Societies of Apostolic Life,* this Dicastery is pleased to give its consent for you to erect the Public Association of the (name of the community), located in your Diocese, as a Religious Institute of Diocesan Right, if you so desire.

The following procedure is to be observed in its erection as an Institute of Diocesan Right.

The lawfully designated Prioress General will make her perpetual profession of vows in your hands or in the hands of a priest delegated by Your Excellency, according to the *formula* indicated in the Constitutions. All the other professed members will make their temporary or perpetual vows in the hands of the Prioress General or in the hands of her delegate, the norms of the universal law of the Church and the Constitutions are to be observed.

Temporary [temporal] goods are to be kept in such a manner that they will have standing in both ecclesiastical and civil law.

Your Excellency, we encourage you to accompany this new religious family with a fatherly concern. We ask that you take special care in ensuring that the Institute has regular General Chapters, during which the sisters can elect their Superior, as foreseen in their Constitutions and in accord with the provisions of canon law. Particular attention must also be given to the rules concerning the administration of the Institute, implemented in regular Chapters of Affairs.

On (date) the Master of (name of the religious family) recognized the Public Association (name of community) as part of the (name of the religious family), we want to recommend, Your Excellency, that this cooperation will always remain vital because with the protection and intercession of St. (name of the founder of the religious family), the Institute can bear abundant fruit.

Finally, we ask you to kindly send a copy of the Decree of Erection of the new Institute and a copy of its approved Constitutions to this Congregation.

In the sincere hope that God will continue to abundantly bless the (name of the community), and the Diocese of (name), we take this opportunity to wish you a blessed and peaceful Christmas.

Sincerely yours in Christ,

(Signed)
João Braz Card. De Aviz
Prefect

(Signed)
P. Sebastiano Paciolla, O.Cist
Undersecretary

DECREE: INSTITUTE OF DIOCESAN RIGHT

Having reviewed the revised Constitution of the (name of the community), a Public Association of the Faithful whose motherhouse is located at (address), and who have been living a more perfect life through the observance of the vows in the spirit of Saint (name of the original founder of the religious family) since 199__; and

Having been given the *nihil obstat* from the Congregation for Religious Institutes and Societies of Apostolic Life on (date) in accordance with canon 579; and

Bearing in mind *Pastor bonus,* Arts. 105, 106 §1, 107, and 108 §1;

I, Bishop (name), decree that the (name of the community) be erected as an Institute of Diocesan Right in the Diocese of (name) in accordance with canon 579; and as the Bishop of the principal seat of this community, I also approve their Constitution in accordance with canons 587 §2 and 595 §1.

Given at the Chancery in (name of the Diocese) on this the ___day of _____ 2013.

Name of Bishop

Name of the Chancellor

CANON 1112

DELEGATION FOR QUALIFIED LAY PERSONS TO ASSIST AT MARRAIGES OF THE FAITHFUL

A diocesan bishop, with the previous favorable vote of the episcopal conference of his territory, requested permission from the Congregation for Divine Worship and the Discipline of the Sacraments to delegate two non-ordained persons the faculty to assist at the marriages of the faithful of the diocese.

UNOFFICIAL ENGLISH TRANSLATION

Prot. N.____
Most Holy Father,

His Most Excellent Lordship _________
Bishop of _________

In light of the scarcity of priests and deacons in his diocese, asks for the permission spoken of in CIC c. 1112 so that he can delegate two religious sisters, of whom mention is made in the episcopal petition, as qualified witnesses of the Church in the territory of his ecclesiastical authority for properly carrying out the liturgical celebrations of marriage in the name of the Church.

THE CONGREGATION FOR DIVINE WORSHIP AND THE DISCIPLINE OF THE SACRAMENTS

By force of the faculties given to it by the Supreme Pontiff Pope John Paul II, in light of the information set forth by the Ordinary and with the previous favorable vote of the Conference of _________ Bishops, kindly assents to the requests set forth and concedes the desired permission, until otherwise provided by this Dicastery, but without prejudice to the prescripts of the Code and in accord with the following explanations and prescriptions, regarding which the Bishop-Petitioner is bound to make each lay person to be delegated aware, namely:

1. This permission is to be held as an entirely extraordinary concession and granted in light of the particular circumstances. Lay persons to be deputed for the duty of assistance at the marriages of faithful must never be considered as "ordinary," since it is of its very nature a supplement, that

is, this duty must not be exercised if there are present priests or deacons who are able and willing to assist in celebrating marriage. Pastors and other priests and deacons are earnestly asked that, imbued with pastoral zeal, they be prepared willingly to exercise their proper liturgical duty in the celebration of each marriage and not absent themselves from it unless legitimately impeded. The presence of lay persons delegated for this duty does not constitute a circumstance exempting priests and deacons from their proper duty.

2. The bishop, either personally or through another priest – through the pastor competent by reason of place if it can be done – is to be made certain that the qualified witness is entirely competent and prepared for giving instruction to those to be married, if this duty is entrusted to the witness, and for worthily carrying out the celebration.

3. General delegation, which is the focus of this rescript, must be conceded in writing (cf. c. 1111 §2) by only the diocesan bishop and those equivalent to him in law, to the exclusion of the vicars general and episcopal vicars unless these are invested with a special mandate.

4. In the document of delegation is to be written the name of the delegated lay person, to whom a determined time of concession is to be assigned. Also to be indicated is the place or places in which the person can exercise the delegation, under penalty of the invalidity of the marriage. The place is to be limited and a circumscription of a parish or several parishes. The delegation is never to be conceded for the whole territory of the diocese.

5. The qualified witness cannot validly subdelegate the delegation so received to others.

6. The delegation expires after the term established in the letters of delegation has elapsed. The delegate is to inform the bishop about this, and the delegate is to return the mandate to him or ask for its renewal.

7. If a priest or deacon lacking the faculty of assisting is present, the delegated lay person is bound to ask him whether he wishes to assist at the marriage. This request causes the effect of delegation conceded by law in this case.

8. The faculty of dispensing from matrimonial impediments, spoken of in cc. 1079-1080, does not pertain to the delegated lay person.

9. The delegated lay person cannot in any way wear the vestments proper

to priests or deacons in carrying out the marriage rite. It is necessary that he or she wears appropriate clothing approved by the Ordinary or only an alb.

10. The delegated lay person is bound to use the rite in the vernacular language that is recognized by the Holy See and prescribed for marriage in that diocese.

11. The qualified witness is to take care that he or she attest to the celebration in marriage in a document, in which are put the signatures of the spouses, witnesses and the qualified witness him/herself, and a document is to be sent as quickly as possible to the pastor of the parish competent for the territory so that he can properly make mention of it in the register of marriages of the parish as is the custom (cc. 1121 §1; 1122).

12. The qualified witness is to warn the contracting parties that they are equally to fulfill the solemnities and prescriptions of civil law.

Given in Rome, at the Halls of the Congregation, ______, 2012

(Signed)
+Antionius Card. Cañizares Llovera
Prefect

Prot. n. 271/12
Beatissime Pater,

Exc. Mus Domine _________
Episcopus _________

Attenta penuria sacerdotum et diaconorum in sua dioecesi, postulat licentiam de qua in can. 1112 Codicis iuris canonici ut dua sorores religiosas de quibus fit mentio in episcopali petitione qua testes qualificati Ecclesiae in territorio sua ecclesiasticae dicionis liturgicis celebrationibus nutpiarium nomine Ecclesiae rite peragendis delegare valeat.

CONGRETATIO DE CULTU DIVINO ET DISCIPLINA SACRAMENTORUM

Vigore facultatum a Summo Pontifice Ioane Paulo PP. II sibi tributarum, attentis ab Ordinario expositis et praehabito voto favorabili Conferentiae Episcoporum _________, precibus expositis benigne annuens petitam licentiam concedit, donec aliter ab ipso Dicasterio praevideatur, firmis tamen praescriptis Codicis et firmis sequentibus rationibus praescriptionisbusque de quibus Episcopus Orator unumquemque laicum delegandum certiorem facere tenetur, scilicet:

1. Licentia haec concessionem prorsus extraordinariam habenda esse et attentis peculiaribus circumstantiis elargita. Laici ad munus nuptiarum fidelium adsistentiae deputandi numquam tamquam <<ordinarium>> haberi debet, quia suae naturae suppletorium, id est haud exercendum si praesto sint sacerdotes vel diaconi qui possint et velint matrimonio celebrando adsistere. Enixe rogantur parochi celterique sacerdotes et diaconi ut, pastorali zelo imbuti, libenter suum proprium munus liturgicum exercendum in celebratione uniuscuiusque matrimonii parati sint neque ab eo se abstineant nisi legitime impediti. Praesentia laicorum ad hoc munus delegati non constituit circumstantiam eximentem sacerdotum et diaconorum a suo proprio munere.

2. Episcopus sive per se sive per alium sacerdotem – per parochum ratione loci competentem si fieri potest – certior sit testem qualificatum ad institutionem nupturientibus tradendam, si hoc munus ipsi concreditur, et ad celebrationem digne peragendam prorsus idoneum et instructum esse.

3. delegatio generalis, de qua in hoc rescripto agitur, scripto est concedenda (cfr. Can. 1111, § 2) ab uno Episcopo dioecesano illique in iure aequiparatis, exclusis Vicariis generalibus et episcopalibus, nisi speciali mandato instruantur.

4. In documento delegationis nomen laici delegati inscribatur, cui tempus determinatum concessionis assignetur. Indicetur quoque locus vel loci in quibus delegationem exercendam potest, sub pena invaliditatis nuptiarum. Locus sit determinatum et paroeciae vel plurium paroeciarum circumscriptum. Delegatio numquam concedatur pro toto territorio dioecesis.

5. Testis qualificatus delegationem receptam valide aliis subdelegare nequit.

6. Delegatio spirat elapso termino in litteris statuto. De hoc delegatus certorem faciat Episcopum cui mandatum remittat vel renovationem eiusdem petat.

7. Si adsit sacerdos vel diaconus facultate assistendi carens, laicus delegatus tenetur illo petendi an velit ipse matrimonio assistere. Quae petitio idem effectum parit delegationis in casu a iure concessae.

8. Laico delegato non competit facultas dispensandi ab impedimentis matrimonialibus, de quibus in cann. 1097-1080.

9. Laicus delegatus nullo modo potest in rito nuptiali peragendo indumenta propria sacerdotum vel diacono rum induere. Vestem dignam ab Ordinario approbatam induat oportet vel solam albam.

10. Laicus delegatus ritum in lingua vernacula a Sancta Sede recognitum et pro matrimonio in illa dioecesi praescriptum uti tenetur.

11. Testis qualificatus curet ut fidem de matrimonio celebrato in documento adsit in quo subsignationes sponsorum, testium ipsuisque testis qualificati apponentur, et documentum quam primum parocho paroeciae competenti pro territorio transmittatur ut in regesto matrimoniorum paroeciae uti de more rite mentionem fiat (cann. 1121 §1; 1122).

12. Testis qualificatus contrahentes admoneat ut pariter sollemnitates praescitionesque legis civilis adimpeant.

Datum Romae, Ex Aedibus Congregationis, ______, 2012

(Signed)
+ Antonius Cardinial Cañizares Llovera
Praefectus

Other Documents

Extraordinary Faculties for the Roman Rota

Pope Benedict XVI, shortly before his resignation as Supreme Pontiff, issued a rescript granting special faculties to the Roman Rota. The special faculties govern internal measures to sensure the timely handling of cases before the Rota.

UNOFFICIAL ENGLISH TRANSLATION

SECRETARY OF STATE
N. 208.966

RESCRIPT *EX AUDIENTIA SS.MI*

Accepting the request presented on 26 January 2013 by His Excellency the Dean of the Roman Rota, Msgr. Pio Vito Pinto, the Supreme Pontiff Benedict XVI, in the Audience granted to the undersigned Cardinal Secretary of State on 11 February 2013, has approved the following special faculties, to be valid for a period of three years:

I. The Rotal sentences which declare the nullity of marriage are executive without the need for a second conforming sentence.

II. It is not possible to propose a recourse before the Roman Rota for a New Proposition of a Cause after one of the parties has contracted a new canonical marriage.

III. There is no appeal against Rotal decisions in the matter of nullity of sentences or of decrees.

IV. The Dean of the Roman Rota has the power to dispense, for a grave cause, from the *Rotal Norms* in a procedural matter.

V. The Rotal Advocates are to be warned about the serious obligation to deal with solicitude the progress of the causes entrusted to them, whether for pay or *ex officio*, such that a process before the Roman Rota not exceed in length a year and a half.

The present Rescript will be published in *Acta Apostolicae Sedis*.

Vatican, 11 February 2013

(Signed)
Tarcisio Card. Bertone
Secretary of State

SEGRETARIO DI STATO
N. 208.966

RESCRIPTUM *EX AUDIENTIA SS. MI*

Accogliendo la richiesta presentata in data 26 gennaio 2013 dall'Ecc.mo Decano della Rota Romana, Mons. Pio Vito Pinto, il Sommo Pontefice Benedetto XVI, nell'Udienza concessa al sottoscritto Cardinale Segretario di Stato l'11 febbraio 2013, ha approvato le seguenti facoltà speciali, da valere per un triennio:

I. Le sentenze rotali che dichiarano la nullità del matrimonio siano esecutive, senza che occorra una seconda decisione conforme.

II. Dinanzi alla Rota Romana non è possibile proporre ricorso per la N.C.P., dopo che una delle parti ha contratto un nuovo matrimonio canonico.

III. Non si da appello contro le decisioni rotali in materia di nullità di sentenze o di decreti.

IV. Il Decano della Rota Romana ha la potestà di dispensare per grave causa dalle Norme Rotali in materia processuale.

V. Siano avvertiti gli Avvocati Rotali circa il grave obbligo di curare con sollecitudine lo svolgimento delle cause loro affidate, sia di fiducia che d'ufficio, cosi che processo davanti alla Rota Romana non ecceda la durata di un anno e mezzo.

Il presente Rescritto verrà pubblicato sugli *Acta Apostolicae Sedis.*

Dal Vaticano, 11 febbraio 2013

(Signed)
†Tarcisio Card. Bertone
Segretario di Stato

Anglicanorum Coetibus

Modifications of the Complementary Norms

In a letter to the Ordinary of the Anglican Ordinariate for the Chair of St. Peter in the United States, the Prefect of the Congregation for the Doctrine of the Faith communicated modifications to Article 1.4 and Complementary Norm 5.1 of the Apostolic Constitution Anglicorum coetibus. *The modification addresses a particular question of who is eligible for membership in the Ordinariate. The changes were confirmed by Pope Francis. The Prefect's letter follow.*

CONGREGATION FOR THE DOCTRINE OF THE FAITH
June 14, 2013
Prot. N. 217/08-43128

Dear Monsignor Steenson,

During the Ordinary Session of this Dicastery held on May 29, 2013, the Cardinal and Bishop Members of the Congregation heard a report on the Personal Ordinariates established under the auspices of the Apostolic Constitution *Anglicanorum coetibus*. Following that report, the Members considered the specific question of the evangelizing mission of the Ordinariate.

The Apostolic Constitution (Article I §4) and the Complementary Norms (Article 5 §1) establish the requirements for canonical membership in the Ordinariate. The question discussed during the aforementioned Ordinary Session was framed this way: *If a baptized Catholic leaves the practice of the faith due to a lack of catechesis, and this person returns to the practice of the faith through the evangelical and catechetical activity of the Ordinariate, could this person become a member of the Ordinariate?*

In responding to this question, it was noted that Article I §4 of the Apostolic Constitution speaks of "Sacraments of Initiation" and not simply "Baptism". It seemed therefore both desirable and possible to modify the current legislation in such a way so as to acknowledge a proper evangelizing mission of the Ordinariate while at the same time respecting the intentionality of *Anglicanorum coetibus*.

Any modification to the Apostolic Constitution or Complementary Norms, however, must be articulated on the basis of objective criteria as membership in the Ordinariate may not be extended for purely subjective motives or personal preference. The reception of all of the Sacraments of Initiation is to be considered the objective sign of an adequate catechesis. Consequently, if a baptized Catholic lacks one or other of the Sacraments of Initiation, and then motivated by the liturgical and pastoral activity of the Ordinariate requests reception of Confirmation or Eucharist, this may be considered an objective criterion allowing canonical inscription in the Ordinariate.

As a result of this discussion, the Members of the Congregation approved modification of Article 5 of the Complementary Norms to the Apostolic Constitution *Anglicanorum coetibus*. This modification was confirmed by the Holy Father, Pope Francis, in an audience granted to me on May 31, 2013, and therefore takes immediate effect. The new formulation of the Complementary Norms read as follows:

Complementary Norms

> 5 §1: The lay faithful originally of the Anglican tradition who wish to belong to the Ordinariate, after having made their Profession of Faith and received the Sacraments of Initiation, with due regard for canon 845, are to be entered in the apposite register of the Ordinariate. Those who have received ***all of the Sacraments of Initiation*** outside the Ordinariate are not ordinarily eligible for membership, unless they are members of a family belonging to the Ordinariate.
>
> ***5 §2: A person who has been baptized in the Catholic Church but who has not completed the Sacraments of Initiation, and subsequently returns to the faith and practice of the Church as a result of the evangelizing mission of the Ordinariate, may be admitted to membership in the Ordinariate and receive the Sacrament of Confirmation or the Sacrament of the Eucharist or both.***
>
> 5 §3: Lay faithful and members of the Institutes of Consecrated Life and Societies of Apostolic Life, when they collaborate in pastoral or charitable activities, whether diocesan or parochial, are subject to the Diocesan Bishop or to the pastor of the place; in which case the power of the Diocesan Bishop or pastor is exercised jointly with that of the Ordinary and the pastor of the Ordinariate.

While this modification does not address all questions and circumstances regarding canonical membership in the Ordinariate, it is my sincere hope that this decision affirms the essential mission of evangelization that is shared by all members of the Church, particularly by those who have embraced the fullness of Catholic communion as the fruit of their longing for the truth.

With prayerful best wishes, I am

Sincerely yours in Christ,

(Signed)
+ Gerhard L. Müller
Prefect

De Caritate Ministranda

Apostolic Letter Issued *Motu Proprio*

ON THE SERVICE OF CHARITY

The service of charity is at the heart of the Church's identity and mission. With this in mind, Pope Benedict XVI addresses the work of charity in and by the Church, and issues new regulations to organize better the Church's charitable activity. De Caritate Ministranda *contains 15 articles governing the diocesan bishop's duties regarding Catholic charitable agencies. The apostolic letter* motu proprio *follows.*

Introduction

"*The Church's deepest nature* is expressed in her three-fold responsibility: of proclaiming the word of God (*kerygma-martyria*), celebrating the sacraments (*leitourgia*) and exercising the ministry of charity (*diakonia*). These duties presuppose each other and are inseparable" (*Deus caritas est*, 25).

The service of charity is also a constitutive element of the Church's mission and an indispensable expression of her very being (cf. *ibid.*); all the faithful have the right and duty to devote themselves personally to living the new commandment that Christ left us (cf. *Jn* 15:12), and to offering our contemporaries not only material assistance, but also refreshment and care for their souls (cf. *Deus caritas est*, 28). The Church is also called as a whole to the exercise of the *diakonia* of charity, whether in the small communities of particular Churches or on the level of the universal Church. This requires organization "if it is to be an ordered service to the community" (cf. *ibid.*, 20), an organization which entails a variety of institutional expressions.

With regard to this *diakonia* of charity, in my Encyclical *Deus Caritas Est* I pointed out that "in conformity with the episcopal structure of the Church, the Bishops, as successors of the Apostles, are charged with primary responsibility for carrying out in the particular Churches" the service of charity (No. 32); at the same time, however, I noted that "the *Code of Canon Law*, in the canons on the ministry of the Bishop, does not expressly mention charity as a specific sector of episcopal activity" (*ibid.*). Although "the *Directory for the Pastoral Ministry of Bishops* explored more specifically the duty of charity as a responsibility incumbent upon the whole Church and upon each Bishop in his Diocese" (*ibid.*), there was still a need to fill the aforementioned lacuna and to give adequate expression in canonical legislation to both the essential nature of the service of charity in the Church and its constitutive relationship with the episcopal ministry, while outlining the legal aspects of this ecclesial service, especially when carried out in an organized way and with the explicit support of the Bishops.

In view of this, with the present *Motu Proprio* I intend to provide an organic legislative framework for the better overall ordering of the various organized ecclesial forms of the service of charity, which are closely related to the diaconal nature of the Church and the episcopal ministry.

It is important, however, to keep in mind that "practical activity will always be insufficient, unless it visibly expresses a love for man, a love nourished by an encounter with Christ" (*ibid.*, 34). In carrying out their charitable activity, therefore, the various Catholic organizations should not limit themselves merely to collecting and distributing funds, but should show special concern for individuals in need and exercise a valuable educational function within the Christian community, helping people to appreciate the importance of sharing, respect and love in the spirit of the Gospel of Christ. The Church's charitable activity at all levels must avoid the risk of becoming just another form of organized social assistance (cf. *ibid.*, 31).

The organized charitable initiatives promoted by the faithful in various places differ widely one from the other, and call for appropriate management. In a particular way, the work of *Caritas* has expanded at the parish, diocesan, national and international levels. *Caritas* is an institution promoted by the ecclesiastical Hierarchy which has rightly earned the esteem and trust of the faithful and of many other people around the world for its generous and consistent witness of faith and its concrete ability to respond to the needs of the poor. In addition to this broad initiative, officially supported by the Church's authority, many other initiatives have arisen in different places from the free enterprise of the faithful, who themselves wish to help in various ways to offer a concrete witness of charity towards those in need. While differing in their origin and juridical status, both are expressions of sensitivity and a desire to respond to the same pressing need.

The Church as an institution is not extraneous to those organized initiatives which represent a free expression of the concern of the baptized for individuals and peoples in need. The Church's Pastors should always welcome these initiatives as a sign of the sharing of all the faithful in the mission of the Church; they should respect the specific characteristics and administrative autonomy which these initiatives enjoy, in accordance with their nature, as a manifestation of the freedom of the baptized.

Alongside these, the Church's authority has, on its own initiative, promoted specific agencies which provide institutionally for allocating donations made by the faithful, following suitable legal and administrative methods which allow for a more effective response to concrete needs.

Nevertheless, to the extent that such activities are promoted by the Hierarchy itself, or are explicitly supported by the authority of the Church's Pastors, there is a need to ensure that they are managed in conformity with the demands of the Church's teaching and the intentions of the faithful, and that they likewise respect the legitimate norms laid down by civil authorities. In view of these requirements, it became necessary to establish in the Church's law certain essential norms inspired by the general criteria of canonical discipline, which would make explicit in this sector of activity the legal responsibilities assumed by the various subjects involved, specifying in particular the position of authority and coordination belonging to the diocesan Bishop. At the same time, the norms in question need to be broad enough to embrace the significant diversity of the institutions of Catholic inspiration which are engaged as such in this sector, whether those originating from the Hierarchy or those born of the direct initiative of the faithful, received and encouraged by the local Pastors. While it was necessary to lay down norms in this regard, there was also a need to consider the requirements of justice and the responsibility of Bishops before the faithful, with respect for the legitimate autonomy of each institution.

Dispositive Part

Consequently, upon the proposal of the Cardinal President of the Pontifical Council *Cor Unum*, and after consultation with the Pontifical Council for Legislative Texts, I establish and decree the following:

Art. 1.

§1. The faithful have the right to join in associations and to establish agencies to carry out specific charitable services, especially on behalf of the poor and suffering. To the extent that these are linked to the charitable service of the Church's Pastors and/or intend to use for this purpose contributions made by the faithful, they must submit their own Statutes for the approval of the competent ecclesiastical authority and comply with the following norms.

§2. Similarly, it is also the right of the faithful to establish foundations to fund concrete charitable initiatives, in accordance with the norms of canons 1303 of the Code of Canon Law (*CIC*) and 1047 of the Code of Canons of the Eastern Churches (*CCEO*). If foundations of this type correspond to the characteristics set forth in Art. 1, they will also observe, *congrua congruis referendo*, the provisions of the present law.

§3. In addition to observing the canonical legislation, the collective charitable initiatives to which this *Motu Proprio* refers are required to follow Catholic principles in their activity and they may not accept commitments which could in any way affect the observance of those principles.

§4. Agencies and foundations for charitable purposes promoted by Institutes of Consecrated Life and Societies of Apostolic Life are required to comply with these norms, and they must follow the prescriptions of canons 312, §2 *CIC* and 575, § 2 *CCEO*.

Art. 2.

§1. The Statutes of each charitable agency referred to in the preceding article must also contain, in addition to its institutional offices and structures of governance in accordance with canon 95, §1 *CIC*, the guiding principles and objectives of the initiative, the management of funds, the profile of its workers, as well as the reports and information which must be presented to the competent ecclesiastical authority.

§2. A charitable agency may use the name "Catholic" only with the written consent of the competent authority, as laid down by canon 300 *CIC*.

§3. Agencies promoted by the faithful for charitable purposes can have an Ecclesiastical Assistant appointed in accordance with the Statutes, according to the norm of canons 324, §2 and 317 *CIC*.

§4. At the same time, the ecclesiastical authority must bear in mind its duty to regulate the exercise of the rights of the faithful in accordance with canons 223, §2 *CIC* and 26, §3 *CCEO*, and thus to avoid the proliferation of charitable initiatives to the detriment of their activity and effectiveness with regard to their stated goals.

Art. 3.

§1. With regard to the preceding articles, it is understood that the competent authority at the respective levels is that indicated by canons 312 *CIC* and 575 *CCEO*.

§2. For agencies not approved at the national level, even though they operate in different Dioceses, the competent authority is understood to be the diocesan Bishop of the place where the agency has its principal office. In any event, the agency has the duty to inform the Bishops of other Dioceses where it operates and to respect the guidelines for the activities of the various charitable agencies present in those Dioceses.

Art. 4.

§1. The diocesan Bishop (cf. canon 134, §3 *CIC* and canon 987 *CCEO)* exercises his proper pastoral solicitude for the service of charity in the particular Church entrusted to him as its Pastor, guide and the one primarily responsible for that service.

§2. The diocesan Bishop encourages and supports the initiatives and works of service to neighbor in his particular Church, and encourages in the faithful the spirit of practical charity as an expression of the Christian life and sharing in the mission of the Church, as indicated in canons 215 and 222 *CIC* and 25 and 18 *CCEO*.

§3. It is the responsibility of the diocesan Bishop to ensure that in the activities and management of these agencies the norms of the Church's universal and particular law are respected, as well as the intentions of the faithful who made donations or bequests for these specific purposes (cf. canons 1300 *CIC* and 1044 *CCEO*).

Art. 5.

The diocesan Bishop is to ensure that the Church enjoys the right to carry out charitable activities, and he is to take care that the faithful and the institutions under his supervision comply with the legitimate civil legislation in this area.

Art. 6.

It is the responsibility of the diocesan Bishop, as indicated by canons 394, §1 *CIC* and 203, §1 *CCEO*, to coordinate within his territory the different works of charitable service, both those promoted by the Hierarchy itself and those arising from initiatives of the faithful, without prejudice to their proper autonomy in accordance with their respective Statutes. In particular, he is to take care that their activities keep alive the spirit of the Gospel.

Art. 7.

§1. The agencies referred to in Article 1, §1 are required to select their personnel from among persons who share, or at least respect, the Catholic identity of these works.

§2. To ensure an evangelical witness in the service of charity, the diocesan Bishop is to take care that those who work in the Church's charitable apostolate, along with due professional competence, give an example of Christian life and witness to a formation of heart which testifies to a faith working through charity. To this end, he is also to provide for their theological and pastoral formation, through specific curricula agreed upon by the officers of various agencies and through suitable aids to the spiritual life.

Art. 8.

Wherever necessary, due to the number and variety of initiatives, the diocesan Bishop is to establish in the Church entrusted to his care an Office to direct and coordinate the service of charity in his name.

Art. 9.

§1. The Bishop is to encourage in every parish of his territory the creation of a local *Caritas* service or a similar body, which will also promote in the whole community educational activities aimed at fostering a spirit of sharing and authentic charity. When appropriate, this service is to be established jointly by various parishes in the same territory.

§2. It is the responsibility of the Bishop and the respective parish priest to ensure that together with *Caritas*, other charitable initiatives can coexist and develop within the parish under the general coordination of the parish priest, taking into account, however, the prescriptions of Article 2, §4 above.

§3. It is the duty of the diocesan Bishop and the respective parish priests to see that in this area the faithful are not led into error or misunderstanding; hence they are to prevent publicity being given through parish or diocesan structures to initiatives which, while presenting themselves as charitable, propose choices or methods at odds with the Church's teaching.

Art. 10.

§1. It is the responsibility of the Bishop to supervise the ecclesiastical goods of the charitable agencies subject to his authority.

§2. It is the duty of the diocesan Bishop to ensure that the proceeds of collections made in accordance with canons 1265 and 1266 *CIC* and canons 1014 and 1015 *CCEO* are used for their stated purposes [cf. canons 1267 *CIC*, 1016 *CCEO*].

§3. In particular, the diocesan Bishop is to ensure that charitable agencies dependent upon him do not receive financial support from groups or institutions that pursue ends contrary to Church's teaching. Similarly, lest scandal be given to the faithful, the diocesan Bishop is to ensure that these charitable agencies do not accept contributions for initiatives whose ends, or the means used to pursue them, are not in conformity with the Church's teaching.

§4. In a particular way, the Bishop is to see that the management of initiatives dependent on him offers a testimony of Christian simplicity of life. To this end, he will ensure that salaries and operational expenses, while respecting the demands of justice and a necessary level of professionalism, are in due proportion to analogous expenses of his diocesan Curia.

§5. To permit the ecclesiastical authority mentioned in Article 3, §1 to exercise its duty of supervision, the agencies mentioned in Article 1, §1, are required to submit to the competent Ordinary an annual financial report in a way which he himself will indicate.

Art. 11.

The diocesan Bishop is obliged, if necessary, to make known to the faithful the fact that the activity of a particular charitable agency is no longer being carried out in conformity with the Church's teaching, and then to prohibit that agency from using the name "Catholic" and to take the necessary measures should personal responsibilities emerge.

Art. 12.

§1. The diocesan Bishop is to encourage the national and international activity of the charitable agencies under his care, especially cooperation with poorer ecclesiastical circumscriptions by analogy with the prescriptions of canons 1274, § 3 *CIC* and 1021 §3 *CCEO*.

§2. Pastoral concern for charitable works, depending on circumstances of time and place, can be carried out jointly by various neighboring Bishops with regard to a number of Churches, in accordance with the norm of law. When such joint activity is international in character, the competent Dicastery of the Holy See is to be consulted in advance. For charitable initiatives on the national level, it is fitting that the Bishop consult the respective office of the Bishops' Conference.

Art. 13.

The local ecclesiastical authority retains the full right to give permission for initiatives undertaken by Catholic agencies in areas of his jurisdiction, with due respect for canonical norms and the specific identity of the individual agencies. It is also the duty of the Bishop to ensure that the activities carried out in his Diocese are conducted in conformity with ecclesiastical discipline, either prohibiting them or adopting any measures needed in cases where that discipline is not respected.

Art. 14.

Where appropriate, the Bishop is to promote charitable initiatives in cooperation with other Churches or Ecclesial Communities, respecting the proper identity of each.

Art. 15.

§1. The Pontifical Council *Cor Unum* has the task of promoting the application of this legislation and ensuring that it is applied at all levels, without prejudice to the competence of the Pontifical Council for the Laity with regard to associations of the faithful as provided for in Article 133 of the Apostolic Constitution *Pastor Bonus*, the competence of the Secretariat of State's Section for Relations with States, and the general competences of other Dicasteries and Institutes of the Roman Curia. In particular, the Pontifical Council *Cor Unum* is to take care that the charitable service of Catholic institutions at the international level is always to be carried out in communion with the various local Churches.

§2. The Pontifical Council *Cor Unum* is also competent for the canonical establishment of charitable agencies at the international level; it thus takes on the responsibilities of discipline and promotion entailed by law.

I order that everything I have laid down in this Apostolic Letter issued *Motu Proprio* be fully observed, notwithstanding anything to the contrary, even if worthy of particular mention, and I decree that it be promulgated by publication in the daily newspaper *L'Osservatore Romano* and enter into force on 10 December 2012.

Given in Rome, at Saint Peter's, on 11 November, in the year 2012, the eighth of my Pontificate.

BENEDICTUS PP XVI

[01602-02.01] [Original text: Latin]

Ministrorum Institutio

Apostolic Letter Issued *Motu Proprio*

WHEREBY THE APOSTOLIC CONSTITUTION *PASTOR BONUS* IS MODIFIED AND RESPONSIBILITY FOR SEMINARIES IS TRANSFERRED FROM THE CONGREGATION FOR CATHOLIC EDUCATION TO THE CONGREGATION FOR THE CLERGY

The training of sacred ministers was one of the chief concerns of the Fathers of the Second Vatican Ecumenical Council, who stated: "The Council is fully aware that the desired renewal of the whole Church depends in great part upon a priestly ministry animated by the spirit of Christ, and it solemnly affirms the critical importance of priestly training" (Decree on the Training of Priests *Optatam Totius*, n. 1). In this context, canon 232 of the Code of Canon Law claims for the Church "the proper and exclusive right" to train those destined for the sacred ministries, a training which ordinarily takes place in seminaries. These are institutions called for by the Council of Trent, which decreed that a *seminarium perpetuum* be set up in all dioceses (Session XXIII [15 July 1563], can. XVIII), so that the bishop might "*alere et religiose educare et ecclesiasticis disciplinis instituere*" candidates for the priesthood.

The first institute of a universal character charged with providing for the establishment, governance and administration of seminaries, "to which the destiny of the Church is closely bound" (Leo XIII, Ep. *Paternae Providaeque* [18 September 1899]: ASS 32 [1899-1900], 214), was the *Congregatio Seminariorum* established by Benedict XIII with the Constitution *Creditae Nobis* (9 May 1725: *Bullarium Romanum* XI, 2, pp. 409-412). With the passage of time this ceased to exist, yet seminaries continued to be the object of particular concern on the part of the Holy See through the Sacred Congregation of the Council (now the Congregation for the Clergy) and the Sacred Congregation for Bishops and Regulars, and, after 1906, through the latter alone. Saint Pius X, with the Apostolic Constitution *Sapienti Consilio* (29 June 1908: AAS 1 [1909], 7-19), reserved jurisdiction over seminaries to the Sacred Consistorial Congregation, in which a specific office was established (cf. AAS 1 [1909] 9-10, 2°, 3).

Benedict XV, with the Motu Proprio *Seminaria Clericorum* (4 November 1915: AAS 7 [1915], 493-495), combined the office for seminaries at the Sacred Consistorial Congregation with the Sacred Congregation for Studies in order to create a new dicastery called *Sacra Congregatio de Seminariis et Studiorum Universitatibus*. As a reason for his decision, the Holy Father mentioned his concern for the increasing number of matters to be dealt with and the importance of the office itself: "*Verum cum apud hanc Sacram Congregationem negotiorum moles praeter modum excreverit, et Seminariorum cum maiorem in dies operam postulet, visum est Nobis ad omnem eorum disciplinam moderandam novum aliquod consilium inire*" (AAS 7 [1915], 494).

The new dicastery, namely, the *Sacra Congregatio de Seminariis et Studiorum Universitatibus*, was included in the 1917 *Codex Iuris Canonici* under canon 256 and the formation of clerics was inserted in the same Code under Title XXI, *De Seminariis*, in Part IV, *De Magisterio Ecclesiastico*, of Book III, *De Rebus*.

It is noteworthy that at the time of the preparation of the new Code there was some question about the appropriateness of maintaining this same arrangement. In the end, however, it seemed more suitable to put the entire body of norms at the beginning of the section dealing with clerics. Consequently the norms and directives on seminaries were inserted in Book II, Part I, Title III, Chapter i, with the appropriate title "The Formation of Clerics" (cf. cann. 232-264 cic). The new arrangement is clearly significant and its title (*De Clericorum Institutione*) is particularly fitting because it now embraces the complete training to be imparted to future ministers of the Lord: a training meant not to be simply doctrinal but also human, spiritual, ascetic, liturgical and pastoral.

The Second Vatican Ecumenical Council also states that "major seminaries are necessary for priestly training" (Decree on the Training of Priests *Optatam Totius,* n. 4) and that the formation imparted in the major seminary is specifically priestly, that is, ordered spiritually and pastorally to the sacred ministry: "the whole training of the students should have as its object to make them true shepherds of souls after the example of our Lord Jesus Christ, Teacher, Priest and Shepherd" (*ibid.*).

Specifically: "young men who intend to enter the priesthood are to be provided with a suitable spiritual formation and prepared for their proper duties in a major seminary throughout the entire time of formation or, if in the judgment of the diocesan bishop circumstances demand it, for at least four years" (can. 235, §1 CIC).

According to the Second Vatican Ecumenical Council and the 1983 Code of Canon Law, then, seminaries are included in the context of "the formation of clerics". If this formation is to be truly effective, it must link ongoing formation to seminary training, since "ongoing formation is a continuation of the formation received in the seminary", as my venerable Predecessor Blessed John Paul II affirmed in his Apostolic Exhortation *Pastores Dabo Vobis* (25 March 1992): "The ongoing formation of priests... is the natural and absolutely necessary continuation of the process of building priestly personality which began and developed in the seminary... with the training program which aimed at ordination. It is particularly important to be aware of and to respect the intrinsic link between formation before ordination to the priesthood and formation after ordination. Should there be a break in continuity, or worse, a complete difference between these two phases of formation, there would be serious and immediate repercussions on pastoral work and fraternal communion among priests, especially those in different age groups. Ongoing formation is not a repetition of the formation acquired in the seminary, simply reviewed or expanded with new and practical suggestions. Ongoing formation involves relatively new content and especially methods; it develops as a harmonious and vital process which — rooted in the formation received in the seminary — calls for adaptations, updating and modifications, but without sharp breaks in continuity. On the other hand, long-term preparation for ongoing formation should take place in the major seminary, where encouragement needs to be given to future priests to look forward to it, seeing its necessity, its advantages and the spirit in which it should be undertaken, and appropriate conditions for its realization need to be ensured" (No. 71: AAS 84 [1992], 782-783).

I therefore consider it fitting to assign to the Congregation for the Clergy the promotion and governance of all that concerns the training, life and ministry of priests and deacons: from the pastoral care of vocations and the selection of candidates for Holy Orders, including their human, spiritual, doctrinal and pastoral training in seminaries and in special centres for permanent deacons (cf. can. 236, §1° CIC), to their continuing formation, including their living conditions and ways of exercising the ministry, as well as their insurance and social assistance.

In the light of the above, after carefully examining all these matters and having sought the opinion of experts, I establish and decree the following:

Art. 1

The *Congregatio de Institutione Catholica* (*de Seminariis atque Studiorum Institutis*) takes the name of *Congregatio de Institutione Catholica* (*de Studiorum Institutis*).

Art. 2

Art. 112 of the Apostolic Constitution *Pastor Bonus* is replaced by the following text: "*The Congregation gives practical expression to the concern of the Apostolic See for the promotion and organization of Catholic education*".

Art. 3

Art. 113 of the Apostolic Constitution *Pastor Bonus* is abrogated.

Art. 4

Art. 93 of the Apostolic Constitution *Pastor Bonus* is replaced by the following text:

"*§1. Without prejudice to the rights of bishops and their conferences, the Congregation examines matters concerning priests and deacons of the secular clergy with regard to their persons and their pastoral ministry, as well as the resources they require for the exercise of this ministry, and in all these matters the Congregation offers appropriate assistance to bishops.*

§2. The Congregation gives practical expression to the concern of the Apostolic See for the formation of those called to Holy Orders".

Art. 5

The text of Art. 94 of the Apostolic Constitution *Pastor Bonus* is replaced by the following:

§1. It assists bishops in ensuring that in their Churches vocations to the sacred ministries are fostered with all possible diligence and that students are suitably educated in seminaries — to be established and directed in accordance with law — and provided with a sound human, spiritual, doctrinal and pastoral formation.

§2. It exercises careful vigilance to ensure that the community life and governance of seminaries fully correspond to the requirements of priestly training and that the superiors and instructors contribute as best they can to the personal formation of sacred ministers by the example of their own lives and sound teaching.

§3. The Congregation is also competent to establish interdiocesan seminaries and to approve their statutes".

Art. 6

The Congregation for Catholic Education is competent to structure the academic curricula of philosophy and theology, after consultation with the Congregation for the Clergy in areas of its respective competence.

Art. 7

The Pontifical Work of Priestly Vocations (cf. Motu Proprio of Pius XII [4 November 1941]) is transferred to the Congregation for the Clergy.

Art. 8

By virtue of the matters treated, the Prefect of the Congregation for the Clergy is *ex officio* President of the Permanent Interdicasterial Commission for the formation of candidates for Holy Orders, established in conformity with the Apostolic Constitution *Pastor Bonus*, Art. 21, §2, of which the Secretary is also a member.

Art. 9

The Interdicasterial Commission for a more equitable distribution of priests in the world is suppressed.

Art. 10

On the day these norms take effect, proceedings pending at the Congregation for Catholic Education involving matters transferred from its competence are to be forwarded to the Congregation for the Clergy for resolution.

I order that all that I have decided in this Apostolic Letter issued *Motu Proprio* is to be fully observed, anything to the contrary notwithstanding, albeit deserving of special mention, and I decree that it is to be promulgated by publication in the daily newspaper *L'Osservatore Romano* and to take effect fifteen days after promulgation.

Given in Rome, at Saint Peter's, on 16 January in the year of our Lord 2013, the eighth of my Pontificate.

BENEDICTUS PP. XVI

[Translation provided by Vatican Website]

FIDES PER DOCTRINAM

APOSTOLIC LETTER ISSUED *MOTU PROPRIO*

WHEREBY THE APOSTOLIC CONSTITUTION *PASTOR BONUS* IS MODIFIED AND COMPETENCE FOR CATECHESIS IS TRANSFERRED FROM THE CONGREGATION FOR THE CLERGY TO THE PONTIFICAL COUNCIL FOR PROMOTING THE NEW EVANGELIZATION

Faith needs to be strengthened *through teaching*, so that it can enlighten the minds and hearts of believers. The particular moment of history in which we are living, marked as it is by a dramatic crisis of faith, calls for an ability to meet the great expectations present in the hearts of believers for a response to the new questions being directed both at the world and at the Church. The understanding of the faith constantly demands that its contents be expressed in a new language capable of presenting, to all who ask, the reason for the hope present in those who believe (cf. 1 Pet 3:15).

It is a particular responsibility of the whole Church to keep the message of Christ ever fresh and effective, also through clear teaching which must nourish faith in the mystery of the incarnation of the Son of God who for our sake became man, died and rose again for our salvation. She must do so tirelessly by appropriate ways and means, so that all those who accept the Gospel message and believe, may be born to new life through baptism.

In this year which marks the 50th anniversary of the beginning of the Second Vatican Council, as the Church meditates upon the rich teaching contained in those documents and finds new ways to implement it, we can acknowledge the great catechetical progress that has been made in these decades. The period after the Council, however, was not without errors, some quite grave, of method and content, which led in turn to deeper reflection and the preparation of a number of post-conciliar documents which have enriched the field of catechesis.

In his Apostolic Exhortation *Evangelii Nuntiandi*, the Venerable Servant of God Paul VI stated that "a means of evangelization that must not be neglected is that of catechetical instruction. The intelligence, especially that of children and young people, needs to learn through systematic religious instruction the fundamental teachings, the living content of the truth which God has wished to convey to us and which the Church has sought to express in an ever richer fashion during the course of her long history" (n. 44: *AAS* 68 [1976], 34).

Blessed John Paul II, concluding the Synod of Bishops devoted to catechesis, also wrote that "within the whole process of evangelization, the aim of catechesis is to be the teaching and maturation stage, that is to say, the period in which the Christian, having accepted by faith the person of Jesus Christ as the one Lord and having given him complete adherence by sincere conversion of heart, endeavors to know better this Jesus to whom he has entrusted himself" (Apostolic Exhortation *Catechesi Tradendae*, 20: *AAS* 71 [1979], 1294).

To celebrate the 20th anniversary of the conclusion of the Second Vatican Ecumenical Council, my blessed Predecessor announced another Synod of Bishops, during which the Synod Fathers expressed their fervent desire that a Catechism be prepared in order to provide the universal Church with a synthetic summary of doctrine and morality in accordance with the Council's indications. With the Apostolic Constitution *Fidei Depositum*, issued on 11 October 1992, Blessed John Paul II promulgated the *Catechism of the Catholic Church* and I myself, with a Motu Proprio dated 28 June 2005, approved and promulgated the *Compendium of the Catechism of the Catholic Church.*

We cannot forget other significant moments in defining the nature, method and ends of catechesis in the process of evangelization. In 1971 the Sacred Congregation for the Clergy issued the *General Catechetical Directory*, as a first synthesis of the progress made in the various local Churches in their own work of catechesis. In 1997, following the publication of the *Catechism of the Catholic Church*, the Congregation for the Clergy issued the *General Directory for Catechesis*, confirming the Church's desire that the first step in catechesis should normally be aimed at conversion (cf. n. 62).

The teaching of the Council and the subsequent magisterium, reflecting the Church's great tradition in this regard, closely linked catechesis to the process of evangelization. Catechesis has a prominent place in the Church's daily life and her tireless efforts to proclaim the word of God to all and to teach believers in Christ to build up his body, the Church (cf. *Catechism of the Catholic Church*, 4).

With the Apostolic Letter issued Motu Proprio *Ubicumque et Semper* of 21 September 2010, I established the Pontifical Council for Promoting the New Evangelization, which pursues its own ends "both by encouraging reflection on topics of the new evangelization, and by identifying and promoting suitable ways and means to accomplish it" (Art. 1 § 2: *AAS* 102 [2010], 791). In a particular way I wished to grant the new Dicastery the task of promoting "the use of the *Catechism of the Catholic Church* as an essential and complete formulation of the content of the faith for the people of our time" (Art. 3, 5°: *AAS* 102 [2010],

792).

Taking all these things into account, I consider it right that this same Dicastery should assume as one of its institutional duties the task of vigilance, to be exercised in the name of the Supreme Pontiff, over that instrument of evangelization which is the Church's catechesis, as well as over the various aspects of catechetical instruction, for the sake of a more organic and effective pastoral activity. This new Pontifical Council can offer suitable help in this regard to the particular Churches and to diocesan bishops.

Therefore, accepting the joint proposal of the Heads of the Dicasteries involved, I have determined that the responsibilities for catechesis, which the Apostolic Constitution *Pastor Bonus* of 28 June 1988 had entrusted to the Congregation for the Clergy, will be transferred to the Pontifical Council for Promoting the New Evangelization, with the same jurisdiction which the former Congregation has hitherto exercised in this area and which is called for in canon law.

Consequently, in light of the above observations and after carefully pondering the matter and having sought the counsel of experts, I establish and decree the following:

Art. 1

Article 94 of the Apostolic Constitution *Pastor Bonus* is abolished and the competence for catechesis hitherto enjoyed by the Congregation for Clergy is entirely transferred to the Pontifical Council for Promoting the New Evangelization.

Art. 2

The International Council for Catechesis established by the Venerable Servant of God Paul VI with a Letter dated 7 June 1973, is likewise transferred to the Pontifical Council for Promoting the New Evangelization. The President of the Pontifical Council will become the president of this Council and the Secretary of the same Dicastery will be a member *ex officio*.

Art. 3

In virtue of the competences granted it by this Apostolic Letter issued *Motu Proprio*, the Pontifical Council for Promoting the New Evangelization:

§1. Is concerned with promoting the religious formation of the faithful of every age and condition;

§2. Has the faculty to issue norms meant to ensure that catechetical instruction is suitably imparted in accordance with the Church's constant tradition;

§3. Has the task of ensuring that catechetical formation is properly carried out with regard to its methods and aims, in accordance with the directives of the Church's magisterium;

§4. Grants the necessary approval of the Apostolic See for catechisms and other writings pertaining to catechetical instruction, with the consent of the Congregation for the Doctrine of the Faith;

§5. Assists the Offices for catechetics within Episcopal Conferences, follows their initiatives pertaining to religious formation which are of an international nature; coordinates their activities and, in certain cases, provides necessary assistance.

What I have established with this Apostolic Letter issued *Motu Proprio*, I wish to be observed fully, now and in the future, anything to the contrary notwithstanding, even if worthy of special mention, and I order it to be promulgated by publication in the daily newspaper *L'Osservatore Romano*, taking effect fifteen days after promulgation.

Given in Rome, at St Peter's, on 16 January in the year of our Lord 2013, the eighth of my Pontificate.

BENEDICTUS PP. XVI

[Translation provided by Vatican Website]

Normas Nonnullas of Benedict XVI

Apostolic Letter issued *Motu Proprio*

ON CERTAIN MODIFICATIONS TO THE NORMS GOVERNING THE ELECTION OF THE ROMAN PONTIFF

With the Apostolic Letter *De aliquibus mutationibus in normis de electione Romani Ponteficis* given as a *Motu Proprio* in Rome on 11 June 2007 in the third year of my pontificate, I established some norms that, rescinding those prescribed in no. 75 of the Apostolic Constitution *Universi Dominici Gregis* promulgated by my predecessor Blessed John Paul II, have re-established the regulation, sanctioned by tradition, according to which a two thirds majority of the votes of the Cardinal electors present is always required for the valid election of the Roman Pontiff.

Considering the importance of ensuring the best implementation of what is concerned, albeit with a different significance, regarding the election of the Roman Pontiff, in particular a more certain interpretation and execution of some provisions, I establish and prescribe that some norms of the Apostolic Constitution *Universi Dominici Gregis*, as well as what I myself set forth in the above-mentioned Apostolic Letter, be replaced with the following norms:

35. "No Cardinal elector can be excluded from active or passive voice in the election of the Supreme Pontiff, for any reason or pretext, with due regard for the provisions of Nos. 40 and 75 of this Constitution."

37. "I furthermore decree that, from the moment when the Apostolic See is lawfully vacant, the Cardinal electors who are present must wait fifteen full days for those who are absent before beginning the Conclave; however, the College of Cardinals is also granted the faculty to anticipated the beginning of the Conclave if all the Cardinal electors are present as well as the faculty to defer, for serious reasons, the beginning of the election for a few days more. But when a maximum of twenty days have elapsed from the beginning of the vacancy of the See, all the Cardinal electors present are obliged to proceed to the election."

43. "From the beginning of the electoral process until the public announce-

ment that the election of the Supreme Pontiff has taken place, or in any case until the new Pope so disposes, the rooms of the *Domus Sanctae Marthae*, and in particular the Sistine Chapel and the areas reserved for liturgical celebrations are to be closed to unauthorized persons, by the authority of the Cardinal Camerlengo and with the outside assistance of the Vice Camerlengo and the Substitute of the Secretariat of State, in accordance with the provisions set forth in the following Numbers."

"During this period, the entire territory of Vatican City and the ordinary activity of the offices located therein shall be regulated, for the period mentioned, in a way that ensures the confidentiality and the free development of all the undertakings connected with the election of the Supreme Pontiff. In particular, provision shall be made, with the help of the Cleric Prelates of the Chamber to ensure that no one approaches the Cardinal electors while they are being transported from the *Domus Sanctae Marthae* to the Apostolic Vatican Palace."

46 §1. "In order to meet the personal and official needs connected with the election process, the following individuals must be available and therefore properly lodged in suitable areas within the confines mentioned in No. 43 of this Constitution: the Secretary of the College of Cardinals, who acts as Secretary of the electoral assembly; the Master of Papal Liturgical Celebrations with eight Masters of Ceremonies and two Religious attached to the Papal Sacristy; and an ecclesiastic chosen by the Cardinal Dean or by the Cardinal taking his place, in order to assist him in his duties."

47. "All the persons listed in No. 46 and No. 55, 2 of this Constitution who in any way or at any time should come to learn anything from any source, directly or indirectly, regarding the election process, and in particular regarding the voting which took place in the election itself, are obliged to maintain strict secrecy with all persons extraneous to the College of Cardinal electors: accordingly, before the election begins, they shall take an oath in the form and using the formula indicated in No. 48."

48. "The persons listed in No. 46 and No. 55 § 2 of this Constitution, having been duly warned about the meaning and extent of the oath that they are to take, before the start of the election process, shall, in the presence of the Cardinal Camerlengo or another Cardinal delegated by him, and in the presence of two numerary participant Apostolic Protonotaries, in due course swear and sign the oath according to the following formula:"

I, N.N., promise and swear that, unless I should receive a special faculty given expressly by the newly-elected Pontiff or by his successors, I will observe absolute and perpetual secrecy with all who are not part of the College of Cardinal electors concerning all matters directly or indirectly related to the ballots cast and their scrutiny for the election of the Supreme Pontiff.

I likewise promise and swear to refrain from using any audio or video equipment capable of recording anything which takes place during the period of the election within Vatican City, and in particular anything which in any way, directly or indirectly, is related to the process of the election itself.

I declare that I take this oath fully aware that an infraction thereof will make me subject to the penalty of automatic (latae sententiae) *excommunication reserved to the Apostolic See.*

So help me God and these Holy Gospels, which I touch with my hand.

49. "When the funeral rites for the deceased Pope have been celebrated according to the prescribed ritual, and everything necessary for the regular functioning of the election has been prepared, on the appointed day of the beginning of the Conclave established in conformity with the provisions of No. 37 of the present Constitution, the Cardinal electors shall meet in the Basilica of Saint Peter's in the Vatican, or elsewhere, should circumstances warrant it, in order to take part in a solemn Eucharistic celebration with the Votive Mass *Pro Eligendo Papa*. This celebration should preferably take place at a suitable hour in the morning, so that in the afternoon the prescriptions of the following Numbers of this Constitution can be carried out."

50. From the Pauline Chapel of the Apostolic Palace, where they will assemble at a suitable hour in the afternoon, the Cardinal electors, in choir dress and invoking the assistance of the Holy Spirit with the chant of the *Veni Creator*, will solemnly process to the Sistine Chapel of the Apostolic Palace, where the election will be held. The Vice Camerlengo, the General Auditor of the Apostolic Camera, and two members of each of the colleges of numerary participant Apostolic Protonotaries, Prelate Auditors of the Roman Rota, and Cleric Prelates of the Chamber will participate in the procession.

51 §2. "It will therefore be the responsibility of the College of Cardinals, operating under the authority and responsibility of the Camerlengo, assisted by the Particular Congregation mentioned in No. 7 of the present Constitution, and with the outside assistance of the Vice Camerlengo and the Substitute of the Secretariat of State, to make all prior arrangements for the interior of the Sistine Chapel and adjacent areas to be prepared, so that an orderly election and its

privacy will be ensured."

55 §3. "Should any infraction whatsoever of this norm occur, those responsible should know that they will be subject to the penalty of excommunication *latae sententiae*, which is reserved to the Apostolic See."

62. "Since the forms of election known as *per acclamationem seu inspiratione* and *per compromissum* are abolished, the form of electing the Roman Pontiff shall henceforth be *per scrutinium* alone."

"I therefore decree that, for the valid election of the Roman Pontiff, at least two thirds of the votes are required, calculated on the basis of the total number of electors present and voting."

64. "The voting process is carried out in three phases. The first phase, which can be called the pre-scrutiny, comprises: 1) the preparation and distribution of the ballot papers by the Masters of Ceremonies—called meanwhile into the Hall together with the Secretary of the College of Cardinals and with the Master of Papal Liturgical Celebrations—who give at least two or three to each Cardinal elector; 2) the drawing by lot, from among all the Cardinal electors, of three Scrutineers, of three persons charged with collecting the votes of the sick, called for the sake of brevity *Infirmarii*, and of three Revisers; this drawing is carried out in public by the junior Cardinal Deacon, who draws out nine names, one after another, of those who shall carry out these tasks; 3) if, in the drawing of lots for the Scrutineers, *Infirmarii* and Revisers, there should come out the names of Cardinal electors who because of infirmity or other reasons are unable to carry out these tasks, the names of others who are not impeded are to be drawn in their place. The first three drawn will act as Scrutineers, the second three as *Infirmarii*, and the last three as Revisers."

70 §2. "The Scrutineers add up all the votes that each individual has received, and if no one has obtained at least two thirds of the votes on that ballot, the Pope has not been elected; if however it turns out that someone has obtained at least two thirds of the votes, the canonically valid election of the Roman Pontiff has taken place."

75. "If the votes referred to in Nos. 72, 73, and 74 of the above-mentioned Constitution do not result in an election, a day will be dedicated to prayer, reflection, and discussion. In subsequent votes, in accordance with the procedure established in No. 74 of this same Constitution, only the two whose names have received the greatest number of votes in the immediately preceding ballot will have the passive electoral right. There can be no waiving of the requirement that

a valid election takes place only by a qualified majority of at least two thirds of the votes of the cardinals who are present and voting. Moreover, in these ballots, the two persons who enjoy the passive electoral right lose their active electoral right."

87. "When the election has canonically taken place, the junior Cardinal Deacon summons into the Hall of election the Secretary of the College of Cardinals, the Master of Papal Liturgical Celebrations, and two Masters of Ceremonies. The Cardinal Dean, or the Cardinal who is first in order and seniority, in the name of the whole College of electors, then asks the consent of the one elected in the following words: *Do you accept your canonical election as Supreme Pontiff?* And, as soon as he has received the consent, he asks him: *By what name do you wish to be called?* Then the Master of Papal Liturgical Celebrations, acting as notary and having as witnesses the two Masters of Ceremonies, draws up a document certifying acceptance by the new Pope and the name taken by him."

All that I have laid down in the Apostolic Letter issued *Motu Proprio* I hereby order to be wholly observed, anything to the contrary notwithstanding.

This document will enter into force immediately upon its publication in the *L'Osservatore Romano.*

This I do decree and establish, notwithstanding any instruction to the contrary.

Given in Rome, at Saint Peter's, on 22 February in the year 2013, the eighth of my Pontificate.

BENEDICTUS PP XVI

[Translation provided by Vatican Website]

Apostolic Letter Issued *Motu Proprio*

ON THE JURISDICTION OF JUDICIAL AUTHORITIES OF VATICAN CITY STATE IN CRIMINAL MATTERS

In our times, the common good is increasingly threatened by transnational organized crime, the improper use of the markets and of the economy, as well as by terrorism.

It is therefore necessary for the international community to adopt adequate legal instruments to prevent and counter criminal activities, by promoting international judicial cooperation on criminal matters.

In ratifying numerous international conventions in these areas, and acting also on behalf of Vatican City State, the Holy See has constantly maintained that such agreements are effective means to prevent criminal activities that threaten human dignity, the common good and peace.

With a view to renewing the Apostolic See's commitment to cooperate to these ends, by means of this Apostolic Letter issued *Motu Proprio*, I establish that:

1. The competent Judicial Authorities of Vatican City State shall also exercise penal jurisdiction over:

a) crimes committed against the security, the fundamental interests or the patrimony of the Holy See;

b) crimes referred to:

-in Vatican City State Law No. VIII, of 11 July 2013, containing *Supplementary Norms on Criminal Law Matters*;

- in Vatican City State Law No. IX, of 11 July 2013, containing *Amendments to the Criminal Code and the Criminal Procedure Code*;

when such crimes are committed by the persons referred to in paragraph 3 below, in the exercise of their functions;

c) any other crime whose prosecution is required by an international agreement ratified by the Holy See, if the perpetrator is physically present in the territory of Vatican City State and has not been extradited.

2. The crimes referred to in paragraph 1 are to be judged pursuant to the criminal law in force in Vatican City State at the time of their commission, without

prejudice to the general principles of the legal system on the temporal application of criminal laws.

3. For the purposes of Vatican criminal law, the following persons are deemed *"public officials"*:

a) members, officials and personnel of the various organs of the Roman Curia and of the Institutions connected to it.

b) papal legates and diplomatic personnel of the Holy See.

c) those persons who serve as representatives, managers or directors, as well as persons who even *de facto* manage or exercise control over the entities directly dependent on the Holy See and listed in the registry of canonical juridical persons kept by the Governorate of Vatican City State;

d) any other person holding an administrative or judicial mandate in the Holy See, permanent or temporary, paid or unpaid, irrespective of that person's seniority.

4. The jurisdiction referred to in paragraph 1 comprises also the administrative liability of juridical persons arising from crimes, as regulated by Vatican City State laws.

5. When the same matters are prosecuted in other States, the provisions in force in Vatican City State on concurrent jurisdiction shall apply.

6. The content of article 23 of Law No. CXIX of 21 November 1987, which approves the *Judicial Order of Vatican City State* remains in force.

This I decide and establish, anything to the contrary notwithstanding.

I establish that this Apostolic Letter issued *Motu Proprio* will be promulgated by its publication in *L'Osservatore Romano*, entering into force on 1 September 2013.

Given in Rome, at the Apostolic Palace, on 11 July 2013, *the first of my Pontificate.*

FRANCISCUS

Advisory Opinions

INTRODUCTORY NOTE

The following opinions were assembled by the members of the Publications Advisory Board from among those submitted to the Society for publication. The opinions carry only the weight of the persons named at the end of each opinion. They do not represent the opinion of the diocese or institution to which the author is affiliated nor of the Canon Law Society of America. Advisory opinions are not authentic interpretations of the law, but reflect the scholarly and practical insights of the contributors.

The opinions are arranged according to the canons of the *Code of Canon Law* and the *Code of Canons of the Eastern Churches*. The original questions have been abbreviated or summarized, and the opinions lightly edited to protect the anonymity of the inquirer and to conform to the style of Canon Law Society of America publications.

The Publications Advisory Board expresses gratitude to the canonists who participated in this year's publication. The continued success of this annual project is a result of their willingness to share their time and talent in service to this important work.

The Canon Law Society of America is interested in receiving opinions that members have formulated in response to specific inquiries, and inquiries in need of responses. It also welcomes the participation of members who wish to be involved in this annual project by offering to render opinions to inquiries received by the Board.

Inquiries or contributions may be directed to:

Canon Law Society of America
Office of the Executive Coordinator
3025 Fourth Street, NE
Suite 111
Washington, DC 20017-1102

CIC Canon 111 §1, *CCEO* Canon 29 §1

Raising Children in Interecclesial Marriages of the Eastern and Latin Churches

In a marriage between a Latin husband and a Maronite wife, can the couple agree to have their child ascribed to the Maronite Church?

Opinion

In the context of this interecclesial marriage, if we were to apply only the provisions of the Latin Code, then *CIC* canon 111 §1 would seem to apply. It states:

> Through the reception of baptism, the child of parents who belong to the Latin Church is enrolled in it; or, if one or the other does not belong to it, both parents have chosen by mutual agreement to have the offspring baptized in the Latin Church. If there is no mutual agreement, however, the child is enrolled in the ritual Church to which the father belongs.

On the basis of this text, John P. McIntyre stated in the 2000 *CLSA Commentary*: "The first paragraph of the canon (111) presents a restrictive norm. Suppose we find a Latin father and an Eastern mother. If both parents agree, can the child be baptized in the Eastern rite? The canon does not permit this. If they both agree, it must be in the Latin Church."[1]

In addition to the 1983 *Codex Iuris Canonici*, Pope John Paul II also promulgated the 1988 apostolic constitution, *Pastor bonus,* regarding the Roman Curia and the 1990 *Codex Canonum Ecclesiarum Orientalium*. On the occasion of presenting the new Eastern Code to the twenty-eighth General Congregation of the Synod of Bishops, John Paul II stated: "In presenting to this Assembly, so representative of the universal Church, the Code which governs the common discipline of all the Eastern Catholic Churches, I regard it as an integral part of

1 John P. McIntyre, "Rite," in *New Commentary on the Code of Canon Law*, eds. John P. Beal et al. (New York, N.Y./Mahwah, N.J.: 2000) 151.

one *Corpus Iuris Canonici*, made up of the above-mentioned three documents promulgated over a period of seven years."[2]

Given this implicit interrelationship of the Codes of the Catholic Church, promulgated by the same legislator, could there not be an Eastern canon that might help answer our question? Indeed, there are nine Eastern canons in which the Latin Church is explicitly addressed.[3] As to the issue of ascription in the context of an interritual marriage, while *CCEO* canon 29 §1 does not name the Latin Church explicitly, it will prove helpful. Eastern canon 29 §1 states:

> A son or daughter who has not completed fourteen years of age is ascribed by virtue of baptism to the Church *sui iuris* to which his or her Catholic father is ascribed; or if only the mother is Catholic, or if both parents are of the same mind in requesting it, to the Church *sui iuris* of the mother, without prejudice to particular law enacted by the Apostolic See.

Unlike the parallel Latin norm, *CCEO* canon 29 §1 is not restrictive in regard to the child's ascription to the Church of the mother if the parents are in agreement in their request. However, one could argue that the Latin Church is not named in Eastern canon 29 §1 and that, as a general rule, the Eastern Code regards all and only the Eastern Catholic Churches *sui iuris*. *CCEO* canon 1 states: "The canons of this Code concern all and only the Eastern Catholic Churches, unless, with regard to relations with the Latin Church, it is expressly (*expresse*) established otherwise."

Until recently, canonists argued regarding the meaning given to *expresse* (expressly) in *CCEO* canon 1. The minority maintained that what is established expressly in the Eastern Code regarding the Latin Church has to be explicit and so they limited the application of the Eastern Code to the Latin Church in relation to only nine canons. On the other hand, the majority argued that what is established in the Eastern Code to oblige or concern the Latin Church can either be explicit or implicit. One of the implicit ways to involve the Latin Church is through the use of the expression "Church *sui iuris*." Although the Latin Church is not a Church *sui iuris* in every sense like an Eastern Catholic Church *sui iuris*, it is in an analogous sense particularly when considered in the context of canons that govern interecclesial relations.

2 *AAS* 83 (October 25, 1991) 490.

3 The nine *CCEO* canons which explicitly regard the Latin Church are: *CCEO* cc. 37; 41; 207; 322; 432; 696 §§1-2; 830 §1; 916 §5; and 1465.

On December 8, 2011, the Pontifical Council for Legislative Texts published an official Explanatory Note regarding *CCEO* canon 1. In that Note, the Council effectively accepted the majority view that the use of the expression "Church *sui iuris*" in the Eastern Code can also imply the Latin Church. While that interpretation does not extend to all the 243 times that the expression appears in the Eastern Code, it certainly does in the context of interecclesial relations. The Note states:

> Consequently, one must hold that the Latin Church is implicitly included by analogy each time that the *CCEO* explicitly uses the term "Church *sui iuris*" in the context of interecclesial relations. We say "by analogy" keeping in mind that the characteristics of the Latin Church, though not coinciding completely with those of the Church *sui iuris* described in canons 27 and 28 §1 of *CCEO*, in this regard, are, nevertheless, substantially similar.[4]

Therefore, given the one *Corpus Iuris Canonici* of the Catholic Church and the Pontifical Council's official Explanatory Note in support, it should be evident that *CCEO* canon 29 §1 can be invoked by the Maronite mother in the context of the interecclesial question raised so that the child can be ascribed to the Maronite Church *sui iuris*, if both parents are of the same mind in requesting it. What is also clear from the Council's Explanatory Note going forward is that canonists will need to be aware that they will more and more likely find applicable Latin legislation outside the Latin Code as the relationship of the Latin Church to the *CCEO* canon 1, and indeed the entire Eastern Code, becomes increasingly defined.

Rev. Jobe Abbass, OFM Conv., JCD

4 *Communicationes* 43 (2011) 315-316.

Canon 290 §3

Commentary on the 'Special Faculties' as Applied to Clerics in Religious Institutes

How are the "Special Faculties" granted to the Congregation for the Clergy in 2009 to be applied to clerics who are incardinated into a religious institute or society of apostolic life?

Opinion

The leadership of a clerical religious institute or society of apostolic life may choose to pursue the dismissal of a member from the clerical state via three new faculties granted to the Congregation for the Clergy by Pope Benedict XVI on January 30, 2009 and announced via a circular letter from the Congregation for the Clergy on April 18, 2009 (Prot. N. 2009 0556):[1]

- Faculty I allows the Congregation for the Clergy to present to the Pope requests for the dismissal from the clerical state of a priest or deacon who has married **or** is guilty of another grave sin against celibate chastity (canons 1394, §1 and 1395, §§1-2).
- Faculty II permits the Congregation to present to the Pope requests to impose perpetual penalties upon a priest or deacon who has engaged in a serious violation of divine or ecclesiastical law (canon 1399).
- Faculty III permits the Congregation for the Clergy to handle requests for the dismissal from the clerical state of a priest or deacon who has voluntarily abandoned ministry for more than five consecutive years.

However, the application of these faculties to religious may not seem obvious upon an initial reading of the text, which is clearly addressed to diocesan bishops. A set of procedural guidelines issued nearly a year later by the Congregation has a similar salutation (Prot. N. 2010 1083). So, how are these special faculties to be utilized in the context of religious clerics?

---

1 Subsequent to the release of this circular letter, the Congregation for the Clergy issued a set of procedural guidelines in March 2010 (Prot. N. 2010 0823). Both of these texts are available at http://www.clsa.org.

First, it is important to recall that the Congregation for the Clergy lacks competence to dismiss a cleric from a religious institute or a society of apostolic life. Therefore, this process must be completed before the matter of dismissal from the clerical state can be considered by the Congregation for the Clergy.

In some situations, dismissal from the religious institute or society of apostolic will have occurred automatically, as in the case of a marriage or notorious defection from the faith (canon 694 §1). In others, the institute or society may turn to canon 695, which provides for a streamlined process to dismiss a religious who has seriously violated celibate chastity. Finally, canon 696 addresses a number of grave causes which may result in dismissal for a religious, utilizing the process detailed in canons 697-699.

The anomaly which arises from utilizing this dismissal process is that, while the cleric is dismissed from the institute/society, he remains in the clerical state. Therefore, while freed from the obligations of the evangelical counsels, he is still bound by the obligations of Orders, including celibacy—but he may not exercise ministry, unless a bishop either receives him or, at a minimum, permits him to exercise ministry (canon 701). So, while dismissal from the institute/society may solve a problem for the institute/society, it may not leave the cleric in an improved situation relative to regularizing his relationship with the Church. Therefore, when possible, it is recommended that both the man's clerical status and his religious standing be addressed canonically. Use of the new faculties is one way to accomplish this goal.

Special Faculty I

The first new faculty gives the Congregation for the Clergy the ability to present to the Pope requests for the dismissal from the clerical state of a priest or deacon who has wed *or* committed another grave sin against celibate chastity.

In each case, the cleric must be given the opportunity to amend his life and, failing that, the chance to petition voluntarily for a dispensation from the obligations of the clerical state. If neither effort is successful, in virtue of this faculty, a canonical trial is not required before the cleric can be dismissed from the clerical state.

The cleric who has allegedly offended against celibate chastity must be notified that the process is taking place, presented with the proofs against him, and given an opportunity to mount a defense, with the assistance of canonical counsel. However, neither the cleric nor his canonical representative should be permitted to bring the process to a standstill by promising a response to the allegation(s) but continuing to delay. Therefore, it is prudent to communicate with the cleric in person or via certified mail, with a return receipt requested from the postal service, so as to confirm the cleric's receipt of notice of the proceedings. In this communication, the cleric should be given a reasonable deadline by which to present any written response he wishes to offer.

After all available evidence has been gathered, including any response made by the priest and/or his canonical counsel, two assessors assist the Ordinary in deciding whether (a) there has been a serious offense against celibate chastity; (b) action against this offense is not precluded under prescription (canon 1362)[2]; and (c) there is no better remedy for the situation other than dismissal from the clerical state.

If all three criteria are met, then a decree to this effect is issued. This decree should summarize the major points of the case, including not only the actions of the cleric but the efforts made to have him abandon his misconduct and live his vocation to Orders with fidelity. If there has been scandal among the faithful, this should also be mentioned explicitly.

Next, this decree is sent to the cleric. The Congregation for the Clergy is sent not only the decree, but the written opinions of the assessors and the major superior, as well as any material utilized to reach these opinions. If additional instruction is required, the Holy See will inform the major superior.

Should dismissal from the clerical state be imposed, it is by the Pope, and there is no appeal.

Special Faculty II

The second of the new faculties allows the Congregation for the Clergy to ask the Pope to impose perpetual penalties upon a cleric who has engaged in a serious violation of divine or ecclesiastical law (e.g., substantial financial misappropriation). This faculty carries with it a derogation from several provisions of the Code of Canon Law, which prohibits the imposition of a perpetual penalty by an administrative process, as well as the imposition of a perpetual penalty for violations of canon 1399 (*see* canon 1317, 1319 §1, 1349, and 1342 §2).

As is the case with Special Faculty I, an administrative process must be conducted locally before the matter is referred to the Congregation for the Clergy.

---

2 It should be noted that, unlike the Congregation for the Doctrine of the Faith in cases involving *graviora delicta*, the Congregation for the Clergy lacks the ability to derogate from prescription.

Should dismissal from the clerical state be imposed, it is by the Pope, and there is no appeal.

Special Faculty III

This faculty permits the Congregation for the Clergy to dismiss from the clerical state priests and deacons who have separated themselves illicitly from the exercise of ministry for at least five continuous years. The Congregation for the Clergy will become involved in these cases only at the request of the cleric's major superior, and such a request can be made only if the major superior has moral certitude that the cleric has abandoned ministry, irreversibly and voluntarily.

In such cases, the cleric may pursue hierarchical recourse, since the decision is rendered by the Congregation for the Clergy and not the Pope. In addition, the cleric later may request readmission to the clerical state from the Congregation for the Clergy, if he finds a bishop willing to present his petition.

Required Personnel

Cases requesting application of these new faculties can only be submitted by the major superior of a clerical religious institute of pontifical right or the major superior of a clerical society of apostolic life of pontifical right.[3] For diocesan religious communities and pontifical communities that are not clerical, collaboration with the appropriate diocesan bishop is necessary. This is not an entirely negative arrangement, in that few religious communities will have the requisite personnel to conduct the necessary canonical process. Therefore, even when reliance upon the diocesan bishop is not required by law, it may be fruitful to the community to have access to diocesan canonical resources.

The local administrative process that must be held to prepare cases of this type requires the participation of a number of parties, all of whom must be priests:

- to ensure that the process takes place in a timely fashion, in accord with the law, the major superior appoints an **instructor**;
- to ensure the right of defense is protected, the accused cleric must be given an opportunity to seek the assistance of **canonical counsel**;
- to aid him in making a decision in each case, the major superior is to appoint and meet with two **assessors**, whose written opinions (based

3 An exception applies to missionary societies of apostolic life (like Maryknoll), as such societies fall under the competence of the Congregation for the Evangelization of Peoples. However, this Congregation was granted similar special faculties on December 19, 2008 (Prot. N. 0579/09).

upon the law and the facts of the case) will be included in the materials sent to the Congregation for the Clergy;

- to ensure the authenticity of all the documents sent to the Congregation, an **ecclesiastical notary** must be named and utilized by the major superior; and
- in cases requesting the application of Special Faculty III, a **promoter of justice** must be named by the major superior; his written opinion is included in the materials sent to the Congregation for the Clergy.

Required Documentation

In applying to utilize these new faculties, the following documentation must be presented, or the major superior must present a detailed explanation as to why any missing documentation is not being provided:

1. the cleric's *curriculum vitae* and an attestation as to his ordination;
2. a copy of the cleric's complete seminary and formation records;
3. if the cleric has married, a copy of his civil marriage certificate;
4. an explanation by the major superior as to why it is extremely difficult or impossible to resolve the matter via another canonical process, coupled with documentation of the pastoral efforts made to have the cleric desist from his misconduct and/or return to ministry;
5. a decree by the major superior initiating the proceedings, in which is included the precise nature of the charges brought against the cleric, the appointment by name of two assessors, an instructor and an ecclesiastical notary;
6. the interrogatory of the cleric <u>or</u> one of the following:
    - an authenticated statement by the cleric demonstrating his awareness of the proceedings and his intention to continue in his misconduct and/or absence from ministry, without seeking dispensation from the obligations of the clerical state; or
    - a document indicating that (i) the whereabouts of the cleric are unknown, coupled with documentation of the efforts made to locate him, or (ii) the cleric is aware of the proceedings and persists in his misconduct and/or refuses to return to ministry, yet is unwilling to participate in the proceedings;

7. the depositions of witnesses and/or experts, as well as copies of the documents summoning these persons to testify and an indication of the means by which these were transmitted;
8. any additional relevant documentation, including proof that all procedural acts were executed by some secure means (e.g., the Postal Service);
9. the decree concluding the instruction of the matter;
10. the *votum* of the Instructor, in which he outlines the course of the investigation and formally transfers the acts to the major superior;
11. the decree of the major superior citing the assessors to gather for consideration of the proofs and the minutes of that meeting, the latter of which must be signed by the major superior and both assessors, detailing the discussion of each allegation and the individual opinion of each assessor;
12. the votum of the major superior, in which he details the facts and arguments in law pertaining to each charge against the cleric and, in cases involving Special Faculty III, an equivalent *votum* from the Promotor of Justice;
13. the petition of the major superior of incardination of the cleric, asking that the Pope accept the case under the provisions of Special Faculty I, II or III.

When this documentation is gathered, it must be authenticated by the notary and indexed, with the pages numbered. Any illegible handwritten documents must be accompanied by a typewritten version. Three bound copies are sent to the Congregation for the Clergy, and one should be retained locally.

Concluding Observations

The fact that each case must be instructed on the local level before the Congregation for the Clergy will consider applying one of the new faculties means that the conduct in question must be able to be proven by gathering supporting testimony and documentation. Therefore, this canonical development is not a remedy for every case involving a problematic religious cleric.

Moreover, the new faculties may be used only when it can be demonstrated, to the satisfaction of the Congregation for the Clergy, that it is impossible or extremely difficult to address the matter by an ecclesiastical trial or an administrative penal process. This may be due to any number of reasons, including a lack of qualified canonical personnel, a lack of adequate financial resources to secure additional canonical assistance, and/or a lack of available substantiation of the alleged offense.

In addition, it is critical to note that these faculties do not apply in situations where there has been an accusation of sexual abuse of a minor. In such circumstances, the provisions of the universal law (*Sacramentorum sanctitatis tutela*) and the any appropriate particular law (such as the *Essential Norms for Diocesan/Eparchial Policies Dealing with Allegations of Sexual Abuse of Minors by Priests or Deacons*) govern, even if the cleric also has, for example, married, abandoned ministry for an extended time or caused grave scandal by his conduct. Thus, the Congregation for the Doctrine of the Faith would be the competent dicastery to handle the matter.

Finally, no major superior is obligated to take advantage of the new faculties, but they may be most useful in American communities seeking to obtain or retain accreditation through Praesidium, as this accreditation does not permit the institute/society to have clerics who are illegitimately absent. Moreover, the Congregation for the Clergy is free to intervene directly when it deems necessary.

Ms. Amy Strickland, JCL

Canon 498

Vote in Establishing the Presbyteral Council by Incardinated Priests Legitimately Outside the Diocese

The statutes of our presbyteral council give our diocesan priests the right to vote, active and passive, in establishing the presbyteral council only if they are living in the diocese. We have several diocesan priests who are legitimately living outside the diocese. They are retired, serving the armed forces, teaching in universities, or working at the Roman curia. None of these has the right to vote in constituting the presbyteral council, and one priest recently questioned if the elimination of this right were valid.

Opinion

The active and passive right of election (*ius electionis*) in constituting the presbyteral council is granted by the Code to "all secular priests incardinated in the diocese" (c. 498 § 1, 1°).[1] This clearly is constitutive law (i.e., law which "constitutes" the presbyteral council) so it cannot be dispensed (c. 86). By virtue of the universal law, these priests have the active and passive right to vote in constituting the presbyteral council; this right is not a grant by the diocesan bishop.[2] The statutes of the presbyteral council (see c. 496) must assure this *ius electionis*.

In the 1977 *Schema*, the antecedent draft of canon 498 § 1, 1° had given the right of election to "all secular priests incardinated in the diocese who at the same time either have a domicile or quasi-domicile in the diocese, or fulfill some office for the good of the diocese" (1977 *Schema* c. 312 §1, 1°). This clearly

1 This same right is also granted *a iure* to "all secular priests not incardinated in the diocese and priests who are members of some religious institute or society of apostolic life, who reside in the diocese and exercise some office for the good of the diocese" (c. 498 § 1, 2°). Indeed, the Complementary Norms of *Anglicanorum coetibus* (4 November 2009) issued by the Congregation for the Doctrine of the Faith explain that priests of the ordinariate can be members of the presbyteral council of the diocese where they provide pastoral care to the faithful of the personal ordinariate: "Article 8. § 1. The presbyters, while constituting the presbyterate of the ordinariate, are eligible for membership in the presbyteral council of the diocese in which they exercise pastoral care of the faithful of the ordinariate (see *CIC*, can. 498, § 2)." The personal ordinariate itself does not have a presbyteral council; instead, a "governing council" replaces both the presbyteral council and the college of consultors (see Apostolic Constitution, *Anglicanorum coetibus*; Complementary Norms, Article 12).

2 The diocesan bishop, however, does have the right to confer active and passive vote in constituting the presbyteral council "on other priests who have a domicile or quasi-domicile in the diocese" (c. 498 § 2). The *ius electionis* is not granted *a iure* to such priests.

excluded secular priests incardinated in the diocese but living elsewhere. On 16 April 1980, the *coetus De populo Dei* determined that incardination in the diocese is sufficient for vote in presbyteral council elections.[3] Consequently, the 1980 *Schema* granted the right of election to all secular priests incardinated in the diocese (1980 *Schema* c. 418 § 1, 1°). This became the promulgated law.

Reflecting on that 1980 *Schema*, Narcís Cardinal Jubany Arnau of Barcelona suggested that passive vote should not be given to secular priests habitually living outside the diocese. The Secretariat did not accept this proposal: it replied that, although secular priests habitually living outside the diocese ordinarily are not elected as members of the presbyteral council, nothing should deprive them of this right.[4] Also reflecting on the same canon, Archbishop Joseph Bernardin of Cincinnati suggested that the conference of bishops determine which priests have active and passive vote; otherwise, abuses could occur (e.g., a priest could be elected who is outside the diocese illegitimately or who has abandoned the ministry). The Secretariat did not accept this recommendation because it could give rise to arbitrariness. Incardinated priests have *per se* the *ius electionis*; however, if they are illegitimately absent or do not exercise the ministry, the diocesan bishop can remove this right.[5]

In view of the foregoing enlightenment on the development of canon 498 § 1, 1°, it is clear that the right of election is enjoyed by all incardinated priests. Statutes issued by the diocesan bishop are unable to eliminate this right. Admittedly, the diocesan bishop can direct the exercise of this right for the common good (e.g., by determining the method of gathering votes, by developing norms for proxy votes, etc.: c. 223 § 2); but such direction cannot eliminate the right of election.

Eliminating the right of election which the law gives to incardinated priests seems to have serious consequences. Arguably, if this right is taken away, the presbyteral council would not be validly constituted; the college of consultors, chosen from among the members of the presbyteral council, would not be validly constituted; actions of the diocesan bishop requiring the consent or counsel of either group would not be valid, etc.

---

3 *Communicationes* 13 (1981) 130.

4 Pontifical Commission for the Revision of the Code of Canon Law, *Relatio complectens synthesim animadversionum ab Em.mis atque Exc.mis Patribus commissionis ad novissimum Schema Codicis Iuris Canonici exhibitarum, cum responsionibus a secretaria et consultoribus datis* (Vatican City: Typis polyglottis vaticanis, 1991) 116.

5 Ibid., 117.

Once again, we see the importance of observing carefully the letter and spirit of canon law as the surest means to preclude confusion among the faithful and harm to the Church.

Rev. Msgr. John A. Renken, STD, JCD

Canons 846 §1 and 889

The Conferral of the Sacrament of Confirmation on Baptized Non-Catholic without the Proper Rite of Reception of Baptized Christians into the Full Communion of the Catholic Church.Opinion

Titus just completed his RCIA and received confirmation during the Easter vigil liturgy in his parish. After listening to a priest's homily in one parish, he became troubled and worried. He started to doubt if his confirmation was validly administered at the Easter vigil by his pastor. He was baptized in an Anglican church (Episcopal Church) many years ago. But he never really practiced his faith in this church. When he went to the university, he met some friends who were Catholics and he hung out with them; and, throughout his university days, he went to the Catholic Church and always received Holy Communion. There was no act of reception into the Catholic Church. After many years, he now decides that he wanted to receive the sacrament of confirmation. He was instructed according to the parish's RCIA program and received confirmation upon completion of the program. But Titus's pastor did not receive him into the church. The pastor just went ahead and administered the sacrament of confirmation, presuming that, since he has been receiving communion in a Catholic church for the past twenty-five years, he must express enough faith to be accepted as a Catholic. But when Titus listened to a homily preached in a friend's parish, he became worried. The priest told the faithful that there are two ways to become a Catholic; one was through baptism in the Catholic Church and the other was through a formal act of reception into the Catholic Church, if the person was validly baptised in another Church or ecclesial community. Titus wants to know if his confirmation was valid, since he was not formally received into full communion of the Church according to the Rite of Reception of Adult. Here is a canonical opinion to address the worry of Titus.

Opinion

We shall first investigate whether Titus was qualified to receive Confirmation. The second inquiry is whether the pastor had the faculty to administer the sacrament of Confirmation on Titus. The third is to ascertain whether confirmation was validly administered to Titus.

The 1983 Code makes the juridical determination of how one can become a Catholic. Canon 11 states that merely ecclesiastical laws bind those baptized into the Catholic Church or those received into it; this means that one can become incorporated into the Catholic Church through the reception of baptism validly administered in the Catholic Church.[1] The second way of becoming a Catholic is through reception into full communion of the Catholic Church. "The Rite of Reception of Baptized Christians into the Full Communion of the Catholic Church" is provided for in the RCIA.[2] Since Titus was already baptized, our inquiry will focus on the second way of becoming a Catholic, namely, whether Titus was received into full communion of the Catholic Church as prescribed by law.

The sacrament of Confirmation is one of the seven sacraments and is to be administered to those who have already received baptism.[3] This is because Baptism is the gateway to all other sacraments.[4] The fact that Titus received valid Baptism in the Anglican Communion, and that he has also expressed his desire to become a Catholic through completing the RCIA program, gives him the right to receive the sacrament of Confirmation.[5] The law stipulates that ministers cannot deny the sacraments to those who seek them and are properly prepared and disposed to receive them.[6]

The bishop is the ordinary minister of Confirmation. Priests are also ministers of Confirmation when granted the faculty by the universal law or by delegation.[7] In regard to the person to be confirmed, priests receive this faculty by virtue of their ecclesiastical office or the mandate of the diocesan bishop. Whenever a priest baptizes a person who is no longer an infant or receives a person who is already baptized into full communion of the Catholic Church, he is given the faculty by universal law to confirm.[8] Given that Titus was already validly baptized, the act of reception of Titus allows any priest receiving him into full communion the faculty to administer Confirmation at the same time. Without the rite of reception, however, such a faculty is not given by universal law to the

1 See c. 204,§1.

2 See *The Rites of the Catholic Church as Revised by the Second Vatican Ecumenical Council,* vol. 1, Prepared by the International Commission on English in the Liturgy A joint Commission of Catholic Bishops Conferences (Collegeville, Minnesota, The Liturgical Press, 1990) nos. 473-499: 275-286 [hereafter *The Rites*]

3 See c. 889, §1.

4 See c. 849.

5 See cc. 213-214.

6 See c. 843 §1.

7 See cc. 882-887.

8 See c. 883, 2.

pastor of Titus, except by delegation or when the candidate is in danger of death.[9] Every baptized person outside the Catholic Church is to be received into full communion before Confirmation.[10] So, it is required that Titus be received into the Church for him to be confirmed. The reception of Holy Communion in the Catholic Church for the past twenty-five years does not make Titus a Catholic. It only means he has been unlawfully receiving Holy Communion, most likely due to his ignorance. This, however, does not suffice for the requirement of a formal act of reception into full communion. Unlawful reception of Holy Communion by a baptized non-Catholic has no juridical effects with regard to the status of the person in the Catholic Church.

The third investigation concerns whether Titus validly received the sacrament of Confirmation. *The Rites of the Catholic Church* no. 479 states: "One who was born and baptized outside the visible communion of the Catholic Church is not required to make an abjuration of heresy, but simply a profession of faith."[11] The profession of faith is all that is required for a valid reception into full communion of the Church. Once this profession of faith is made, Titus becomes fully incorporated into the Catholic Church and therefore qualified to receive confirmation.

Titus was never told that he needed to make this profession of the faith in order to become a Catholic. The liturgical law requires that "the person to be received into full communion should be consulted about the form of reception."[12] This requirement enables the candidate to be properly disposed to formulate the right intention to become a Catholic. It also ensures an adult cannot be forced against his or her will to become a Catholic.[13] The decision must be a free act, consciously made by the candidate. In other words, baptized non-Catholics do not become Catholics by accident or by attending Catholic liturgical ceremonies alone. The right intention and free will must be present for reception into full communion to take place. Since Titus was never formally received by a rite of reception into full communion, could it be possible that he never formulated the intention to become a Catholic? There is no doubt that Titus intended to become

9 See c. 883, 3.

10 See c. 889 §1. There is one exception to this rule: someone baptized in an Orthodox Church would also normally have been validly confirmed at the same time.

11 *The Rites*, p. 276.

12 Ibid., no. 475, p. 275.

13 The Fathers of the Second Vatican Council taught explicitly that human dignity requires that nobody should be forced to accept any religious faith. See THE SECOND VATICAN COUNCIL Declaration on Human Freedom *Dignitatis Humanae*, Augustine FLANNERY, (gen. ed.), *Vatican Council II: The Conciliar and Post-Conciliar Documents*, new rev. ed., vol. 1 (Northport, New York, Costello Publishing Co., 1996) 2: 800.

a Catholic; otherwise, he would not have been registered for the RCIA program. But intention alone is not enough; the legal formalities for the reception must also be observed.[14] However, the renewal of baptismal promises made during the Easter vigil will suffice for the requirement to make a profession of faith.[15] The renewal of baptismal promises is also an expression or profession of faith in the Catholic Church.

Conclusion

The conferral of the sacrament of Confirmation on Titus by his pastor was valid, albeit illicit.[16] The minimum requirement of profession of faith through renewal of baptismal promises supplies for the formal profession of faith and the formal reception by the pastor as prescribed in the law. Laws that grant favours are to be broadly interpreted.[17] In this light, a broad interpretation is to be given to what is understood as "to make a profession of faith" in order to be received into full communion.

Rev. Edwin N. Omorogbe, JCD

---

14 Cf. c. 124 §1.

15 See c. 889 §2.

16 In celebrating the Sacraments, the law prescribes that every minister is obliged to observe the rites in the liturgical books. They are not to add or omit or alter anything in them. Titus's pastor has no right to have omitted the rite of reception. This is why we consider his act unlawful. See c. 846 §1.

17 See *Regulae Iuris*, no. 15.

Canon 983 §1

Certificates of First Reconciliation

On the day following the First Confession of the school and religious education students, Father Smith, the recently appointed pastor of Saint Anthony Parish, finds on his desk a stack of "Certificates of First Reconciliation." Accompanying the certificates is a memo from the Director of Religious Education asking Father Smith to sign the certificates, as the former pastor always did. Is Father Smith free to do this?

Opinion

Father Smith is not free to sign these certificates. To do so he must either violate canon 983 §1 himself or require another confessor to do so.

If Father Smith was the confessor of the student-penitents, by signing their certificates he is directly and publicly revealing the identity of the penitents. This, I argue, is a clear violation of the requirements of canon 983 §1 which states that "it is absolutely forbidden (*nefas*) for a confessor to betray in any way a penitent in words or in any manner and for any reason." If Father Smith was not the confessor, how does he ascertain that the one whose name is on the certificate truly made a confession? Is it enough to know that the child attended the Rite of Penance? Does he verify with the DRE or the child's catechist that the child went into the confessional where one of the parochial vicars was hearing confession? The mere fact that the child went into the confessional does not prove that the child made a sacramental confession. There is the possibility – no matter how remote – that the child did not make a true confession. Alternatively, does Father Smith ask the parochial vicar if the child made a sacramental confession? If he answers affirmatively, the parochial vicar is revealing the identity of the penitent to the pastor so that he, in turn, can reveal the penitent's identity by signing a certificate of first reconciliation. In this instance, of course, the pastor who was not the confessor is not bound by the requirements of canon 983 §1, but undoubtedly the parochial vicar is.

It is the opinion of this author that the so-called certificates of first reconciliation cannot and should not ever be used. Any attestation that a specific person made a sacramental confession will – in one fashion or another – require the confessor to violate canon 983 §1 by revealing the identity of the penitent. It should be noted that the canons never call for the recording of the reception of the Sacrament of Penance. (On a related matter, I would argue that priests should not record Confession in the parish register of visitation to the sick, nor should publishers include Confession alongside Anointing of the Sick, Viaticum, etc. in these registers.)

Surprisingly, some approved religious education textbooks for First Penance include a "Certificate of First Reconciliation" as a keepsake for the child. It is the opinion of this author that the certificates should be removed before these textbooks are allowed to be used in class. It is bad pastoral practice to use these certificates, even if they do not call for the pastor's signature. Anything that identifies a penitent – even for the purpose of commemorating a significant moment in faith formation – threatens the penitent's confidence in the seal of confession and its inviolability. The bishop or other ecclesiastical authority who granted an *imprimatur* or *nihil obstat* to a textbook containing a certificate of first reconciliation should immediately revoke that permission. It is the duty of the ecclesiastical authority who wrongly granted the permission to notify the publishing house of the revocation and the reasons why it is being done. He should also give the publisher an opportunity to amend the text by removing the certificate so as to qualify for publication. Finally, pastors should not purchase so-called "Certificates of First Reconciliation" nor should Catholic publishing houses or retailers sell them.

Rev. Msgr. Michael A. Souckar, JCD

Canon 994

Granting Indulgences to an Orthodox Christian

In accord with canon 844 §3, a priest visiting a hospital hears the confession of, anoints, and administers Viaticum to a dying Orthodox man. He also grants the Apostolic Pardon to the dying man after absolution. Now, he is wondering if he acted properly. May the Apostolic Pardon be given to non-Catholics in such a situation?

Opinion

What is called the "Apostolic Pardon" in the English translation of the Ritual is actually a plenary indulgence.[1] A literal translation of the Latin text of the formula makes this plain: "By a faculty given me by the Apostolic See, I grant you a plenary indulgence and the remission of all sins in the name of the Father, and of the Son, and of the Holy Spirit. Amen." The faculty in question is granted by a rubric of the Roman Ritual.[2]

Canon 994 states: "Any member of the faithful (*quivis fidelis*) can gain partial or plenary indulgences or apply them to the dead by way of suffrage." The expression "any faithful" means any baptized person, which is explicit in a norm of the *Enchiridion indulgentiarum*: "To be capable of gaining indulgences a person *must be baptized*, not excommunicated, and in the state of grace at least at the time the prescribed works are completed."[3] The Orthodox and other non-Catholic Christians are capable of gaining an indulgence; they are no longer considered excommunicated due to schism or heresy, as they were under the former law. However, a subsequent norm of the *Enchiridion* adds the following:

---

1 *Pastoral Care of the Sick: Rites of Anointing and Viaticum* (Washington, International Commission on English in the Liturgy, 1982) no. 201.

2 "Sacramentum Paenitentiae vel actus paenitentialis concludi potest indulgentia plenaria in articulo mortis, quam sacerdos infirmo hoc modo concedit: Ego, facultate mihi ab Apostolica Sede tributa, indulgentiam plenariam et remissionem omnium peccatorum tibi concedo, in nomine Patris, et Filii, et Spiritus Sancti. Amen." *Rituale Romanum: Ordo unctionis infirmorum eorumque pastoralis curae*, 7 December 1972 (Typis Polyglottis Vaticanis, 1972) no. 106.

3 *Enchiridion indulgentiarum: normae et concessiones*, 4th ed., 16 July 1999 (Libreria Editrice Vaticana, 1999) no. 17, §1: "Ut quis capax sit lucrandi indulgentias debet esse baptizatus, non excommunicatus, in statu gratiae saltem in fine operum praescriptorum."

"In order that a capable person may actually gain indulgences, it is required that he or she must have at least the general intention to acquire them."[4]

A Catholic may be presumed to have at least the general, or habitual, intention of acquiring an indulgence at the time of imminent death. This can hardly be said of the Orthodox faithful, as indulgences are not part of the Eastern tradition. In the Eastern Code, not a single canon is devoted to indulgences, unlike the Latin Code which has a separate chapter with six canons (cc. 992-997). Likewise, other non-Catholic Christians either ignore or formally reject the theology and practice of indulgences. Thus, it may be presumed that a baptized non-Catholic does not have a habitual intention of acquiring indulgences. This presumption may surely yield in particular cases, but this is not one of them. It is highly unlikely that this dying, hospitalized man even knew that the priest was imparting an indulgence; and possibly the priest himself did not know this either, given his reliance on the approved English translation of the Ritual which inexplicably obfuscates this fact. Consequently, the indulgence in this case was not effective due to the lack of the required intention on the part of the recipient.

As a general rule for pastoral practice, the answer to the question that has been posed must be negative. Due to the necessity of having at least the habitual intention to acquire the indulgence, it should not be granted to baptized non-Catholics unless, in accord with the condition in a parallel place in the law, they "would ask on their own for it" (*sponte id petant*; cf. c. 844 §3).

Dr. John M. Huels, JCD

---

4 "Ut vero subiectum capax eas lucretur, habere debet intentionem saltem generalem eas acquirendi ...." (no. 17, §2).

Canon 1041

Irregularity for Holy Orders

Canon 1041, 2°-6° lists several actions that, by their commission, render one receiving holy orders 'irregular.' While these irregularities are ecclesiastical law and as such do not bind non-Catholics, it is uncertain how these irregularities apply to non-Catholics who are subsequently baptized into the Catholic Church or are received into it. When they enter into full communion, they become bound by canon 1041 and all ecclesiastical laws. If non-Catholics commit acts before they become Catholic that would have rendered them irregular, do they become irregular when they subsequently enter into full communion?

Opinion

Canon 1041 delineates various actions that can give rise to an irregularity for the reception of orders. The issue is whether an irregularity can arise only by a person who has been baptized into the Catholic Church or received into it and is subject to ecclesiastical law (c. 11). Because only persons in full communion with the Church can commit the delicts of heresy, apostasy, and schism (c. 751), non-Catholics cannot incur the irregularity listed in canon 1041, 2°.

The remaining irregularities (c. 1041, 3°-6°) arise from actions which can also be committed by non-Catholics. The counterpart to this canon, *CCEO* canon 762, contains a second paragraph that declares that one incurs an impediment (irregularity) only when the action is gravely sinful, external, and perpetrated after baptism. This restriction does not clarify the issue since the baptism could have taken place outside the Catholic Church.

The actions that give rise to irregularities can be violations of divine, natural, divine positive or ecclesiastical law; however, the attendant irregularity is a provision of ecclesiastical law. Further, canon 1041 restricts the right of a generally qualified male to be considered as a candidate for sacred orders (cf. *CIC* cc. 1029, 1031-1032). Because of the restrictive and exceptive nature of the provisions regarding irregularity, they are to be interpreted strictly (*CIC* c. 18).

A strict interpretation leads to the conclusion that a person can incur an irregularity only if he commits the acts while in full communion and thus is subject to the ecclesiastical law that establishes the irregularity. A personal history that includes such behavior, while not carrying an irregularity with it, should nonetheless be evaluated when assessing a candidate's suitability for sacred orders.

Mr. Matthew Orzolek, JCL

Canon 1044 §1, 3°

Priest as an Accomplice in an Abortion

"What is the status and ability to function of a priest who encouraged his pregnant partner to have an abortion?"

Opinion

An abortion "is the deliberate and direct killing, by whatever means it is carried out, of a human being in the initial phase of his or her existence, extending from conception to birth."[1] The procurement of an abortion is not a crime reserved to the Apostolic See, but religious guilty of such a delict are to be dismissed (c. 695) and priests incur an irregularity or permanent impediment for the exercise of ministry (c. 1044 §1, 3°). If a priest incurs a *latae sententiae*, undeclared excommunication, because of involvement with an abortion,[2] any bishop or priest could absolve the properly disposed priest from the censure of excommunication in the internal forum.

Before any canonical penalties are imposed by an administrative process or a penal trial, there normally needs to be a preliminary investigation.[3] This means that the facts of the case and the imputability of the cleric have been properly documented.[4] This documentation is important whether there is a penal trial or an administrative process.

If a case becomes public knowledge[5] in the media, and the bishop declares

---

1 Pope John Paul II, Encyclical, *The Gospel of Life* (25 March, 1995), no. 58.

2 Canon 1398.

3 Congregation for the Clergy, Prot. No. 37937/05 CA, June 23, 2007: quoted in Francis Morrisey, OMI, "Violations of Canon 277 (with an Adult) Appropriate and Just Responses," *The Canonist* 1(2010) 2, 62.

4 Patrick R. Lagges, "The Penal Process: The Preliminary Investigation in Light of the Essential Norms of the United States," in P. Cogan, ed., *Sacerdotes iuris*, (Ottawa, Saint Paul University: 2005) 255-296.

5 The 1983 Code does not define "public" but the 1917 Code c. 2197 stated: "A delict is public, if it is already known or is in such circumstances that it can be and must be prudently judged that it will easily become known; 2. Notorious by notoriety of law, [if it is] after a sentence by a competent judge that renders the matter an adjudicated thing, or after confession by the offender made in court in accord with canon 1750; 3. Notororius by notoriety of fact, if it is publicly known and was committed under such circumstances that no clever evasion is possible and no legal opinion could excuse [the act]; 4. Occult, if it is not public; materially occult, if the delict

that the priest is excommunicated because of his cooperation[6] with the woman having an abortion, then according to canon 1355[7] it is the Ordinary who initiated the trial to impose or declare the penalty, or the Ordinary that declared the penalty by decree, or the Ordinary of the place where the offender lives who may remit an imposed or declared excommunication. Of course, the power to remit the censure may be delegated.

If an offending priest with an undeclared censure finds it hard to remain in a state of serious sin while waiting for the competent superior to make provision, then canon 1357 allows for any priest to grant absolution. However, the penitent must have recourse to the competent superior within one month or the penalty is reincurred.[8] This canon does not apply if the penalty was declared or imposed.

The crime of being an accomplice in an abortion means that the priest is irregular for the exercise of orders: Canon 1044 §1. "The following are irregular for the exercise of orders received...No. 3 a person who has committed a delict

---

is hidden; formally occult, if imputability [is not known]," translation Edward Peters, *The 1917 Pio-Benedictine Code of Canon Law*, (San Francisco: Ignatius Press, 2001).

6 Canon 1329 §2. Accomplices who are not named in a law or precept incur a latae sententiae penalty attached to a delict if without their assistance the delict would not have been committed, and the penalty is of such a nature that it can affect them; otherwise, they can be punished by *ferendae sententiae* penalties.

7 Canon 1355 §1. Provided that the penalty has not been reserved to the Apostolic See, the following can remit an imposed or declared penalty established by law:

1° the ordinary who initiated the trial to impose or declare a penalty or who personally or through another imposed or declared it by decree;

2° the ordinary of the place where the offender is present, after the ordinary mentioned under n. 1 has been consulted unless this is impossible because of extraordinary circumstances.

§2. If the penalty has not been reserved to the Apostolic See, an ordinary can remit a *latae sententiae* penalty established by law but not yet declared for his subjects and those who are present in his territory or who committed the offense there; any bishop can also do this in the act of sacramental confession.

8 Canon 1357 §1. Without prejudice to the prescripts of canons 508 and 976, a confessor can remit in the internal sacramental forum an undeclared latae sententiae censure of excommunication or interdict if it is burdensome for the penitent to remain in the state of grave sin during the time necessary for the competent superior to make provision.

§2. In granting the remission, the confessor is to impose on the penitent, under the penalty of reincidence, the obligation of making recourse within a month to the competent superior or to a priest endowed with the faculty and the obligation of obeying his mandates; in the meantime he is to impose a suitable penance and, insofar as it is demanded, reparation of any scandal and damage; however, recourse can also be made through the confessor, without mention of the name.

§3. After they have recovered, those for whom an imposed or declared censure or one reserved to the Apostolic See has been remitted according to the norm of canon. 976 are also obliged to make recourse.

mentioned in canon 1041, nn. 3, 4, 5, 6."[9] The irregularity can arise through being an accomplice in an abortion.[10]

To incur the irregularity for the exercise of orders, the priest would have to have been involved in supporting or encouraging the abortion. His cooperation could have been "physical or moral, by requesting, counselling, or urging the abortion."[11] The irregularity must be interpreted in the light of canon 18 because laws restricting people's rights are subject to a strict interpretation.[12] So the involvement of the priest in the abortion must have been a deliberate, sinful action to incur the irregularity as a positive co-operator.

If a priest had donated sperm which could have ultimately led to unused foetuses being disposed of, he would probably not incur the irregularity.[13] A donor would usually have not thought about this possibility, and would have not have been consulted or even told about the disposal of the unused foetuses. The irregularity would not be incurred if the ordained impregnated a woman and she had an abortion without his involvement or agreement.[14]

Canon 1047 identifies who can dispense from impediments and irregularities. Whenever the fact of the irregularity has been in the judicial forum, canonical or secular,[15] either in a marriage nullity or criminal case, then the dispensation is reserved to the Holy See.

The Apostolic Penitentiary is competent for all occult cases of abortion. The Congregation for Institutes of Consecrated Life and Societies of Apostolic Life is competent to deal with cases of the irregularity in non-occult cases involv-

---

9 Canon 1041. "The following are irregular for receiving orders: No. 4. A person who has committed voluntary homicide or procured a completed abortion and all those who positively cooperated in either."

10 Canon. 1329 §2. Accomplices who are not named in a law or precept incur a latae sententiae penalty attached to a delict if without their assistance the delict would not have been committed, and the penalty is of such a nature that it can affect them; otherwise, they can be punished by ferendae sententiae penalties." http://www.vatican.va/archive/ENG1104/__P4W.HTM.

11 William Woestman, OMI, *The Sacrament of Orders and the Clerical State* (Ottawa: Saint Paul University, 1999), 69.

12 Canon 18. "Laws which establish a penalty, restrict the free exercise of rights, or contain an exception from the law are subject to strict interpretation." http://www.vatican.va/archive/ENG1104/__P3.HTM accessed 11 July 2011.

13 C.f. Paul Golden, "Canon 1041, 4 Irregularity for Orders after In Vitro Fertilization," in S. Euart, J. Alesandro and P. Hartmann, Editors, *Roman Replies and CLSA Advisory Opinions 2010* (Washington DC: Canon Law Society of America, 2010) 146-148.

14 Woestman, *The Sacrament of Orders and the Clerical State*, 69; cf. Holy Office, decree, *Redeuntibus*, October 25, 1918: *CLD* 1: 98-103.

15 Woestman, 81.

ing religious. The Congregation for Divine Worship and the Discipline of the Sacraments is competent for all other non-occult cases.[16]

Capacity of the Priest to Minister

If a priest incurred a *latae sententiae* excommunication because of his necessary involvement with an abortion, he would be prohibited from receiving and celebrating sacraments (c. 1331). A priest with an irregularity, who attempts to exercise the orders received, celebrates the sacraments validly but illicitly. This means that the effect of the impediment or irregularity is similar to that of a priest's being suspended as far as the celebration of the Eucharist is concerned.

When the censure of excommunication has been declared, the prohibition to celebrate the sacrament is suspended whenever a member of the faithful is in danger of death,[17] or at any time when a member of the faithful of his or her own accord asks to receive a sacrament.[18]

Every person, including a priest, has a right to a good reputation (c. 220). A person does not have to reveal publicly the commission of a crime preventing them from receiving or celebrating a sacrament. A *latae sententiae* excommunication applies in the internal forum, so "there can be no obligation to observe it in the external forum."[19] Consequently, canon 1352 §2 provides that "The obligation to observe an undeclared *latae sententiae* penalty which is not notorious in the place where the offender is present, is suspended totally or partially whenever the offender cannot observe it without danger of grave scandal or infamy."

Since abortion is a matter of divine law, the Church must uphold the sanctity of life in all circumstances, using all means at its disposal including penalties especially when a priest is involved.

Rev. Brendan P. Daly, JCD

---

16 See *Pastor bonus*.

17 Canon 1352 §1. If a penalty prohibits the reception of the sacraments or sacramentals, the prohibition is suspended as long as the offender is in danger of death.

18 Canon 1335. If a censure prohibits the celebration of sacraments or sacramentals or the placing of an act of governance, the prohibition is suspended whenever it is necessary to care for the faithful in danger of death. If a *latae sententiae* censure has not been declared, the prohibition is also suspended whenever a member of the faithful requests a sacrament or sacramental or an act of governance; a person is permitted to request this for any just cause.

19 Juan Arias, in A Marzoa, J. Miras and R. Rodrigues-Ocana, Editors, *Exegetical Commentary on the Code of Canon Law*, Vol. IV/1 (Montreal, Wilson & Lafleur: 2004) 1052.

Canon 1121

The Obligation of the Parish Priest to Proper Recording of Names in Marriage Register

A pastor in our diocese recently died. It was discovered that for several years he had not conducted (or at least retained) pre-nuptial investigations for marriages celebrated in the parish and had not recorded these marriages in the appropriate registers. People have begun to come to get certificates. Can these marriages be recorded in the registers now? And, if so, under what conditions?

Opinion

Canon 1121 §1 directs:

> After a marriage has been celebrated, the pastor of the place of celebration or the person who takes his place, even if neither assisted at the marriage, is to note as soon as possible in the marriage register the names of the spouses, the person who assisted, and the witnesses, and the place and date of the celebration of the marriage.

This directive is only one of several in the Code of Canon Law which imposes obligations on pastors and others to record events, especially sacramental events that pertain to the canonical status of the members of the faithful.[1] Sometimes the canons underscore the seriousness of this obligation by stipulating that the pastor is to record these matters "carefully" (*sedulo*) and promptly (*sine ulla mora, quam primum*). Unfortunately, some pastors are remiss in fulfilling their responsibility to record marriages and other significant events in the appropriate registers; and their negligence is not discovered until years after the fact. What, if anything, can be done to make up for a pastor's failure to make required entries in the parish registers?

Although canon 1121 charges pastors to record marriages in the parish "as soon as possible" after their celebration, it seems clear that the expression *quam primum* is inserted to emphasize the seriousness of the obligation, not to preclude recording of marriages later if the pastor has neglected his responsibility. Nor

1 See c. 535 on required parish registers; cc. 877-878 on recording baptism; cc. 894-896 on recording the reception of confirmation; cc. 1053-1054 on recording ordinations; cc. 1121-1122 on recording marriages; c. 1123, cc. 1685 and 1706 on recording declarations of nullity and dissolutions of marriage, as well as any attached vetita; c. 1182 on recording deaths.

does the law limit the events that can be recorded in the parish registers to those which are (eventually) reported to the pastor by the official minister or witness of the event. Canon 878 stipulates that, when a baptism is not administered by or in the presence of the pastor, "the minister of baptism, whoever it is (*quicumque est*), must inform the pastor" so that he can record the event. The clause *quicumque est* is a somewhat oblique reference to the possibility that the baptism may have been administered by a lay person either lawfully in the situation of danger of death or validly but unlawfully in other circumstances (c. 861 §2). When a Catholic is granted a dispensation from the observance of the canonical form to enter a marriage with a non-Catholic, the Catholic "is bound to notify as soon as possible" the local ordinary who granted the dispensation and the pastor of his or her place of residence so that the marriage can be duly recorded (c. 1121 §3). In a similar way, when a marriage is legitimately celebrated according to the "extraordinary form," "the priest or deacon who was present at the celebration, or otherwise the witnesses *in solidum* with the contracting parties are bound to inform as soon as possible the pastor or local ordinary about the marriage entered into" (c. 1121 §2). As canon 841 §3 of the *CCEO* and c. 1103 §3 of the 1917 code make explicit, the purpose of this notification of the pastor of the celebration of marriage according to the extraordinary form is so that he can see that it is recorded in the appropriate registers.

The Church's law is concerned not only that information about marriages and other events affecting the status of the faithful be recorded but that it be recorded accurately. Thus, pastors must be certain that they have accurate information about a marriage or other sacramental event before they enter it into the parish registers. Canon 876 states that, as long as it is not prejudicial to anyone's interests, the testimony of one witness who is "above all exception" (*omni exceptione maioris*) or even of the one baptized himself if he was baptized in adulthood is sufficient. If the ordinary minister who performed the baptism was available to attest to its occurrence, he would be a "qualified witness," i.e., one who testifies about what he did in his official capacity (c. 1573) and his testimony would provide full proof even if the fact of the baptism was prejudicial to someone's interests. By contrast, a witness *omni exceptione maior* is simply a legitimate witness, one judged to be "of ordinary honesty and perception." Such a witness "above all exception" could be the lay person who baptized in unusual conditions or even someone who was present at the event. Before recording a baptism performed in the parish by someone other than himself, the pastor should ascertain from the witness the date of the baptism and the names of the child, the minister, the parents and the sponsors, if any. If the minister was not an ordinary one, it might be prudent to assure that the rite involved the pouring of water and the prescribed form as well.

The law seems to require a somewhat higher level of certainty before a marriage not celebrated in the presence of the pastor is recorded in the parish registers. Obviously, if the one reporting the information about the celebration to the pastor is the priest or deacon who assisted in the name of the Church, he is a "qualified witness" whose testimony alone is sufficient to provide the certainty required to record the facts in the registers. The testimony of the one who married following a dispensation from the observance of canonical form is also sufficient for the pastor to record information about the marriage itself, the place of celebration, the public form employed, and the dispensation received (c. 1121 §3). However, canon 1121 §2 stipulates that the priest or deacon who assisted at an extraordinary form celebration or the two witnesses and the spouses *in solidum* are to inform the pastor of the marriage so that it can be duly recorded. The *in solidum* testimony of the witnesses and the spouses may be a precaution to allow the pastor to determine that the conditions for resorting to the extraordinary form had, in fact, been met before he proceeded to record the event. At the least, no more proof should be required for the recording of a marriage celebrated according to canonical form but not recorded in the registers at the time by the pastor.

If the recording of the marriage was neglected by the pastor at the time of its celebration, a certified copy of the civil marriage record, a public civil document, gives full proof of the information contained therein (c. 1541). In the absence of a public document or in the case the information it contains is incomplete, the spouses and original witnesses' testimony, either *in solidum* or separately, about the celebration should provide sufficient certainty about the facts surrounding the celebration to permit the belated recording of the marriage in the parish registers. If the original witnesses are unavailable, the testimony of others who were present at the celebration can be accepted as long as they are "above all suspicion." Although the code gives greater weight to the *viva voce* testimony of witnesses than to written and sworn affidavits, the pastor has considerable leeway in determining the probative weight to be attributed to affidavits and other essentially private documents. In most cases, these affidavits of those who were present at the original celebration when taken together with the testimony of the parties should provide more than ample assurances for the pastor to record the information in the parish books.

The law of the Church requires the registering of marriages and other such events to insure that there will be a public ecclesiastical record of the status of the faithful in the Church. It would defeat the purpose of the law to require greater proof that a sacrament was celebrated than is usually required for the declaration of nullity before the event is recorded in the parish books.

Rev. John P. Beal, JCD

Canon 1127 §2

Dispensation from the Observance of Canonical Form by the Local Ordinary

Michael, a Catholic, and Gretchen, a Lutheran, have approached their parish priest about marriage. They plan to seek a dispensation from the observance of the canonical form so that they can marry in Gretchen's Lutheran church with her step-father, a Lutheran pastor, as officiant. In the course of the pre-nuptial investigation, it is discovered that Gretchen was baptized in the Catholic Church as an infant at the insistence of her Catholic father. While she was still an infant, her parents divorced and her mother remarried a Lutheran. All of Gretchen's religious formation has been in the Lutheran church where she was eventually confirmed and she has always considered herself a Lutheran. Can Michael's local ordinary grant the dispensation from the observance of the canonical form or is this dispensation reserved to the Holy See?

Opinion

Canon 1127 §2 authorizes the local ordinary of the Catholic party to a mixed marriage to dispense the Catholic from the obligation of observing the canonical form so that the wedding can be validly and licitly celebrated in the presence of a non-Catholic minister or a civil official. In 1985, the Pontifical Commission for the Interpretation of the Code of Canon Law, as it was then known, ruled that, outside situations of danger of death, local ordinaries could not dispense from the observance of the canonical form for the marriages of two Catholics; such dispensations are reserved to the Holy See, as they have been at least since Paul VI's 1966 motu proprio *De Episcoporum muneribus*.

The authorization of the local ordinary to dispense from the obligation of observing canonical form in cases of mixed marriages is not, however, an innovation of the 1983 code. The authorization had been introduced into ecclesiastical law by Paul VI's 1970 motu proprio *Matrimonia mixta* which totally reorganized the Church's discipline governing mixed marriages. The legislation of *Matrimonia mixta* on dispensations from the obligation to observe the canonical form of marriage was incorporated virtually without change into the 1983 Latin code. In 1972, the Pontifical Commission for the Interpretation of the Decrees of Vatican II was asked whether the authority of the local ordinary to dispense from the obligation of observing the canonical form extended to the case of a Catholic who wished to marry a person who "was, indeed, baptized in the Catholic Church but later defected from the faith and was converted to another confession which is not Catholic." The Commission's response was: "In the affirmative." [A.A.S. 64 (1972) 397; CLD 7: 750] Since the provisions of the revised code simply repeat the post-conciliar discipline of *Matrimonia mixta*, this authentic interpretation should govern the case of Michael and Gretchen. (c. 6 §2)

Some have cited the Council for Legislative Texts 2006 circular letter "Actus Formalis Defectionis" as a reason why the 1972 authentic interpretation is no longer applicable. The intent of this circular letter was to clarify the requirements for the "act of formal defection from the Catholic Church" mentioned in canons 1086, 1117 and 1124 of the 1983 code, which exempted those baptized in or received into the Catholic Church from certain ecclesiastical laws. The circular letter made clear that this "act of formal defection" required "a) the internal decision to leave the Catholic Church; b) the realization and external manifestation of that decision; and c) the reception of that decision by the competent ecclesiastical authority." By these criteria, Gretchen's defection to the Lutheran church did not qualify as an act of formal defection. However, the issue is not whether Gretchen is bound by the obligation of observing canonical form but whether Michael's local ordinary is empowered to dispense from the obligation. Moreover, as the circular letter insists, defection from the Catholic Church by a formal act "is new to canonical legislation and is distinct from the other—rather 'virtual' (that is deduced from behaviors-- forms of 'notoriously' or 'publicly' abandoning the faith." The letter cites canons 171 §1, 4°; 194 §1, 2°; 316 §1; 694 §1, 1°; and 1071 §1, 4° and §2, most of which echo the provisions of the 1917 code, as examples of such non-formal or "virtual" defection. By these standards, Gretchen did indeed defect from the Catholic Church.

Since this kind of non-formal or "virtual" defection from the Catholic Church was familiar to canonists in 1972 and since defection "by a formal" act did not enter the canonical vocabulary until 1983, it is the former that the Pontifical Council for the Interpretation of the decrees of Vatican II had in mind when they held that the local ordinary can dispense from the obligation of observing canonical form to permit the marriage of a Catholic and a person who was baptized in the Catholic Church but later defected from it. This conclusion is confirmed by two similar authentic interpretations by the Commission concerning the faculty of presbyters to confirm baptized adults whom they receive into full communion in virtue of office or mandate. The Commission held that the faculty to confirm did extend to the "readmission of an apostate to the faith who had never been confirmed" [April 25, 1975, *A.A.S.* 67 (1975) 348; CLD 8: 475] and to admit into full communion one who "had already been validly baptized in the Catholic Church but who afterwards, without fault, was brought up in a non-Catholic religion or adhered to it" [December 21, 1979, *A.A.S.* 72 (1980) 105; CLD 9: 527-528]. In both of these cases, people baptized in the Catholic Church who had defected from it without meeting all the requirements for defection by a formal act were considered equivalent to non-Catholics for the purpose of the exercise of a faculty granted by the law. Since the law governing the faculty of presbyters to confirm in the 1983 code simply restates the law of the *Rite of Confirmation*, §7 and the *Order for the Valid Admission of the Already Baptized into Full Communion*, §8, the authentic interpretations based on the earlier law retain their force (c. 6 §2). There is no reason that the pre-code authentic interpretation of the authority of the local ordinary to dispense from the observance of canonical form for a mixed marriage when one of the parties is a Catholic and the other, although baptized in the Catholic Church, later drifted and defected from it should be treated any differently.

If Gretchen were seeking admission to full communion with the Catholic Church, there is no doubt that the presbyter who received her into full communion could also confirm her at that time. It seems equally clear that Michael's local ordinary has the authority to dispense from the observance of canonical form so that Michael's marriage to Gretchen in the Lutheran church with her father officiating can be recognized as valid by the Catholic Church.

Rev. John P. Beal, JCD

Canon 1210

The Appropriate Use of Sacred Places

The president of a Catholic university recently announced that the chapel will be available for rental by external groups. The chapel is rather ornate and it is presumed that it will be an attractive venue for holding meetings, conferences, and other events. The revenue generated from the rental of the chapel will assist with alleviating the operating budget deficit. Some members of the university community have expressed concerns about the rental of the chapel for these purposes. What can be done in these circumstances?

The Code of Canon Law treats several types of sacred places, including churches (cc. 1214-1222), oratories and private chapels (cc. 1223-1229), shrines (cc. 1230-1234), altars (cc. 1235-1239), and cemeteries (cc. 1240-1243). In common parlance, the terms "church," "oratory" and "chapel" are frequently used interchangeably which can be a source of confusion. A church is "a sacred building designated for divine worship to which the faithful have the right of entry for the exercise, especially the public exercise, of divine worship" (c. 1214). An oratory is "a place for divine worship designated by permission of the ordinary for the benefit of some community or group of the faithful who gather in it and to which other members of the faithful can also come with the consent of the competent superior" (c. 1223). A private chapel is "a place for divine worship designated by permission of the local ordinary for the benefit of one or more physical persons" (c. 1226).

The term "chapel" as it is used in the question above is most appropriately classified as an "oratory" in the Code of Canon Law.[1] It is not for the benefit of one or more physical persons but for the use of a group of the faithful – the university community. Before granting permission for the establishment of an oratory, the *ordinary* must visit the place, either personally or through another, so as to ensure that it has been properly prepared (c. 1224 §1; cf. c. 134 §2). This permission is most appropriately conveyed by means of a singular decree since it makes a provision for the good of the community (c. 48). After this permission

1 If the university was established before 1983, the chapel would have been properly classified as a semi-public oratory (cf. *CIC*/1917, c. 1192). The 1917 Code distinguished three types of oratories: public, semi-public, and private or domestic (*CIC*/1917, c. 1188). The latter now corresponds with a private chapel in the 1983 Code, whereas the distinction between public and semi-public is no longer made (cf. c. 1223).

has been granted, an oratory cannot be converted to profane use without the authority of the same ordinary (c. 1224 §2). If the oratory is blessed according to the rite prescribed in the liturgical books, which is entirely fitting (c. 1229), it becomes a sacred place (c. 1205).[2]

In the event that an oratory has been blessed, and consequently made a sacred place, "anything not consonant with the holiness of the place is forbidden" (c. 1210). This means that an oratory may only be used for the exercise or promotion of worship, piety, or religion. It is nonetheless possible for the ordinary, *in individual cases*, to permit other uses which are not contrary to the holiness of the place, such as the use of a sacred place as a shelter in cases of disaster or emergencies, or, in some cases, for religious services of non-Catholic Christians.[3]

In the event that an oratory has not been blessed, there are still restrictions on its use for purposes other than divine worship.[4] Once permission has been given by the ordinary for the establishment of an oratory, it cannot be converted to profane use without the authority of the same ordinary (c. 1224 §2). Similarly, oratories – even those that are not blessed – "must be reserved for divine worship alone and free from all domestic uses" (c. 1229). The ordinary could, however, permit other uses which are not contrary to the holiness of the place, *in individual cases*, as stated in c. 1210.[5] Consequently, we can identify a two-fold restriction on the use of an oratory for profane uses: its designation as an oratory by the ordinary, applicable to all oratories; and its being a sacred place, in the event that

2 The appropriate blessing to be used is found in the Roman Pontifical, specifically Chapter V of the *Ordo dedicationis ecclesiae et altaris*, editio typica, 29 May 1977 (Typis Polyglottis Vaticanis, 1977). The competent minister of blessing is the *ordinary* or his delegate (see c. 1207).

3 For sharing space with non-Catholic Christians, see the 1993 *Ecumenical Directory*, nn. 103, 137-142. The Ecumenical Directory, n. 137 states: "Catholic churches are consecrated or blessed buildings which have an important theological and liturgical significance for the Catholic community. They are therefore generally reserved for Catholic worship. However, if priests, ministers or communities not in full communion with the Catholic Church do not have a place or the liturgical objects necessary for celebrating worthily their religious ceremonies, the diocesan bishop may allow them the use of a church or a Catholic building and also lend them what may be necessary for their services."

4 The 1917 Code, c. 1196, did not allow private or semi-private oratories to be blessed, other than to receive the common blessing of places and houses. This common blessing (*Benedictio loci vel domus*) can be found in the 1952 *Rituale Romanum*, Tit. IX, cap. VI, n. 3. Although this invocative blessing was not obligatory, private and semi-public oratories needed to be reserved solely for divine worship and free from all domestic use (*CIC*/1917, c. 1196 §2).

5 This is not explicit in the law itself, but, as Huels argues, if an ordinary can permit a *sacred place* to be used for purposes that are not contrary to the holiness of the place, i.e., those which have been blessed or dedicated in accordance with the law, he can surely do so for an oratory that has been designated, but not blessed, by the ordinary. (J.M. Huels, "Sacred Places and Times [cc. 1205-1253]," in J. Beal, J. Coriden, and T. Green [eds.], *New Commentary on the Code of Canon Law*, commissioned by the Canon Law Society of America (New York and Mahwah, NJ, Paulist Press, 2000) 1436.

it has been blessed according to the rite prescribed in the liturgical books.

Once designated, all sacred celebrations can be performed in legitimately established oratories except those which the law or a prescript of the local ordinary excludes or the liturgical norms prohibit (c. 1225).[6] The Blessed Sacrament may not, however, be reserved in an oratory without obtaining the additional permission of the *local ordinary* (c. 934 §1, 2°; cf. c. 134 §1).[7] The appropriate use of an oratory is not determined by the presence or absence of the Blessed Sacrament but in virtue of its designation as an oratory. Pledging to remove the Blessed Sacrament in the event that the oratory is to be used for secular purposes is a wholly inadequate solution. Even if the Blessed Sacrament is reserved in a side chapel or other suitable place, either on a permanent or temporary basis, the oratory itself remains restricted from profane use.

In light of its designation as an oratory, a university chapel may not be rented to external groups for the purpose of holding meetings, conferences, or other events. Oratories are restricted from domestic use, even if the Blessed Sacrament and other sacred furnishings are removed. It would seem that the university president is left with three options, two of which require the intervention of the ordinary. Firstly, the university president may seek permission from the ordinary, *in individual cases*, to permit other uses which are not contrary to the holiness of the place.[8] Permission for indiscriminate use by external groups cannot be granted; each request must be assessed on its own merits. Secondly, and most drastically, the university president may request from the ordinary a permanent reduction of the oratory to profane use. In other words, the university chapel would no longer be designated as such; the space could then be used for purposes unrelated to divine worship. A decree of the competent ordinary (cf. c. 1212; 1224 §2) would be required.[9] This is not an arbitrary decision,

6 Some sacred functions are especially entrusted to the pastor (c. 530); see also cc. 857-859; 881; 932-964; 1011; 1118; 1179.

7 This additional permission is not required for a church or oratory connected to the house of a religious institute or society of apostolic life, where the Blessed Sacrament must be reserved (c. 934 §1, 1°).

8 The Congregation for Divine Worship prepared directives on concerts in churches. These are to be occasional events and the ordinary is to grant the permission *per modum actus*. To preserve the sacred character of the church, the ordinary can specify that: permission must be requested in writing; a fee must not be charged; the concert must be open to all; the performers and audience must be dressed in an appropriate manner; the musicians and singers must not be placed in the sanctuary; the Blessed Sacrament should be reserved in a side chapel (n. 10). See CONGREGATION FOR DIVINE WORSHIP, Circular letter regarding music concerts in churches, 5 November 1987, in *Notitiae*, 24 (1988) 3-10, English translation in *CLD* 12: 714-720.

9 Besides the ordinary, it would be advantageous to consult the diocesan bishop. It is the diocesan bishop's responsibility to ensure suitable pastoral care is provided to students of Catholic univer-

motivated exclusively by financial exigency. As a Catholic university, it is not unreasonable for the university community to expect a suitable place of worship, a practical and permanent demonstration of its faith and institutional identity.[10]

The third, and perhaps most difficult option, is to retreat entirely from this proposition. Recognizing the importance of maintaining a suitably designated chapel, the university president may be able to identify other spaces for rental that will achieve a similar financial objective. Catholic universities are reminded of the obligation to provide effective pastoral ministry to members of the university community, that is, an opportunity "to integrate religious and moral principles with their academic study and non-academic activities, *thus integrating faith with life*" (*Ex corde Ecclesiae*, n. 38).

> As a natural expression of the Catholic identity of the University, the university community *should give a practical demonstration of its faith in its daily activity,* with important moments of reflection and of prayer. Catholic members of this community will be offered opportunities to assimilate Catholic teaching and practice into their lives and will be encouraged to participate in the celebration of the sacraments, especially the Eucharist as the most perfect act of community worship (*Ex corde Ecclesiae*, n. 39).

The ability to provide these opportunities for personal and communal prayer is compromised without a fitting place of worship. Where it already exists, a suitably designated chapel should be preserved as an essential characteristic of the institutional identity of a Catholic university, not as a multi-purpose space available for the indiscriminate and crass use of those in search of conference facilities.

Dr. Chad J. Glendinning, JCD

---

sities (c. 813). Similarly, diocesan bishops are the directors, promoters and guardians of the entire liturgical life in the church entrusted to their care (c. 835 §1).

10 *Ex corde Ecclesiae* notes that "besides the teaching, research and services common to all Universities, a Catholic University, by *institutional commitment,* brings to its task the inspiration and light of the *Christian message.* In a Catholic University, therefore, Catholic ideals, attitudes and principles penetrate and inform university activities in accordance with the proper nature and autonomy of these activities. In a word, being both a University and Catholic, it must be both a community of scholars representing various branches of human knowledge, and an academic institution in which Catholicism is vitally present and operative." John Paul II, Apostolic Constitution on Catholic Universities *Ex corde Ecclesiae*, 15 August 1990, n. 14, in *AAS* 82 (1990) 1475-1509, English translation in *Origins* 20 (1990) 265-276.

Canon 1342

Determining which Procedure to Follow When There is an Alleged Crime which is not a More Grave Delict

Your bishop is faced with an ecclesiastical crime which he cannot avoid addressing using a penal process. He is asking his diocesan canonist who was probably involved already as the preliminary investigation unfolded to help him address the question in c. 1718 §1, 3°: "whether a judicial process must be used or, unless the law forbids it, whether the matter must proceed by way of extrajudicial decree." What should guide the diocesan canonist as he advises his bishop?

Opinion

In this matter, one must not follow the norms regarding cases reserved to the Congregation for the Doctrine of the Faith; in this non-reserved case, the Code and only the Code must be followed and the key canon which must be considered is c. 1342, especially §§ 1 and 2:

> §1. Whenever just causes preclude a judicial process, a penalty can be imposed or declared by extrajudicial decree; penal remedies and penances, however, can be applied by decree in any case whatsoever.
>
> §2. Perpetual penalties cannot be imposed or declared by decree, nor can penalties be so applied when the law or precept establishing them prohibits their application by decree.

What one should immediately notice is the Latin Code's clear preferential option for using the judicial process. This notion was discussed during the revision of the Code, and the *coetus de delictis et poenis* clearly rejected any movement to place the administrative penal process (also called the extrajudicial process) on an equal footing ("*aequo iure*") with the judicial process. It is interesting to note in this regard that the framers of the Eastern Code *(CCEO)* were even more emphatic with their stressing the use of the judicial process for the application of penalties. Canon 1402 §1 of the *CCEO* states clearly: "*Any contrary custom being reprobated*, a canonical penalty must be imposed through a penal trial prescribed in cc. 1468 – 1482…" (Emphasis added). Although the Eastern Code does allow the use of the administrative penal process, it requires a grave cause standing in the way of using the judicial trial before the administrative approach is allowed, as one can see in the text of c. 1402 §2 of the *CCEO*:

> C. 1402 §2: If, however, in the judgment of the authority mentioned in §3, there are grave causes that preclude a penal trial and the proofs concerning the delict are certain, the delict can be punished by an extra-judicial decree according to the norm of cann. 1486 and 1487, provided it does not involve a privation of office, title, insignia or a suspension for more than one year, demotion to a lower grade, deposition or major excommunication.

The more important matter to be kept in mind here is that, according to the law of both Codes, one may use the administrative penal process only if there is some cause which actually stands in the way (*obstent/obstant*) of using the judicial trial to apply a penalty. It is particularly interesting that this text has sometimes been interpreted as meaning there are present just causes (or grave causes) positively suggesting the use of the administrative procedure. In reality, both Codes are saying that the causes (just or grave) look to those situations wherein the judicial process cannot or should not be used. In other words, the choice to use the administrative penal process is not to be based upon the issue of convenience but upon the presence of a cause (either just or grave, depending on the code in question) which serves as an obstacle to the use of the judicial trial.

Another factor which might guide the application of c. 1342 is that the 1973 penal law *schema* of this canon (c. 28) stated that before the administrative penal process could be used, not only would grave causes have to stand in the way of using the judicial process but the preliminary investigation must have surfaced "evident proofs of a delict" ("*probationes de delicto evidentes sint*"). It is equally interesting that the *CCEO* also retained this same provision in c. 1402 §2.

It would be difficult to mount a successful argument that the dioceses in the USA are unable to constitute a tribunal for a penal trial. It is well known that trials of this sort have taken place for some time now. Even the Congregation for the Doctrine of the Faith has been asking bishops in this country to establish the Congregation's own tribunal of second instance for more grave delict cases and to pick the judges and the promoter of justice.

The law is clear in c. 1342 §2 that in order to apply perpetual penalties the Ordinary has no choice other than to use the judicial process. If the bishop has in view a dismissal of a cleric or the imposition or declaration of an excommunication, then he must use a collegiate tribunal (c. 1425,§1, 2°). Although c. 1425 §2 would not require a collegiate tribunal for the imposition of a lesser penalty, given the complexity of many penal cases, the bishop might be well advised to follow the recommendation of this canon and entrust the case to a collegiate tribunal.

In the case at hand, it should be evident to the Ordinary whether or not he is seeking to apply a perpetual penalty. Of course, he cannot do so unless the law regarding the particular delict allows for the infliction of such a penalty. If the law states that a just penalty may be applied, this is an indeterminate penalty and, according to c. 1349, the Ordinary may not seek a perpetual penalty for the offender. In addition, even if the Ordinary might have threatened a penalty by way of a penal precept, according to c. 1319 he would not be able to threaten the application of a perpetual penalty. Thus, unless the Code itself provides for the possibility of a perpetual penalty, the Ordinary cannot inflict one on an offender. Canon 1317 states that particular law cannot establish the perpetual penalty of dismissal from the clerical state. Thus, there are various restrictions on the establishment and application of perpetual penalties.

In this particular case, the Ordinary is not faced with a delict reserved to the Holy See. The only delicts not reserved to the Holy See for which the *CIC* provides the possible option of dismissal from the clerical state are the following:

- a cleric who attempts marriage, even if only civilly and who, after being warned does not repent, continues to offend and to give scandal (c. 1394);
- a cleric who persists after a warning to live in concubinage, other than the case mentioned in canon 1394, and the cleric who, after a warning, persists with scandal in another external sin against the sixth commandment of the Decalogue (c. 1395 §1);
- a cleric who has committed an offense against the sixth commandment of the Decalogue, if the delict was committed by force or threats or publicly and with persons other than minors under the age of 18 (c. 1395 §2).

According to the *CCEO*, the hierarch can address the following delicts not reserved to the Holy See with the possible option of what is called *deposition* which is equivalent in the Latin Code to dismissal from the clerical state:

- a cleric who has committed a homicide is to be punished with a major excommunication[1] in addition to other penalties, not excluding deposition (c. 1450 §1). (Note that the application of the penalty of major excommunication also requires the use of the judicial trial according to c. 1402 §2);
- a cleric who persists in living in concubinage or otherwise persists in an external sin against chastity causing scandal *may be* punished with deposition (c. 1453 §1);
- a cleric who has attempted a forbidden marriage *must be* deposed (c. 1453 §2); this penalty is obligatory, yet according to canon 1409 §1 the judge still has options such as deferring the application of the penalty or issuing a lighter penalty as long as the goals of penal law are reached;
- anyone who has approached the civil authority directly or indirectly to obtain by its intervention sacred ordination, an office, a ministry or another function in the Church, is to be punished with an appropriate penalty not excluding major excommunication, which would require a trial, and, in the case of a cleric, even deposition which also would require a trial (c. 1460).

Conclusion

The canonist-advisor of an Eastern Rite hierarch would counsel that a judicial trial would be necessary in most cases in light of the very strong preferential option for the judicial process as expressed in canon 1402 of the CCEO. As the canonist-advisor of a Latin Rite bishop can see from the above discussion, employing a judicial trial also would seem to be advised more often than not and even in addressing those ecclesiastical crimes for which it is not possible to apply a perpetual penalty. The rationale is the fact that it is very often a complex matter to determine whether or not a crime has been committed and to provide for the right of defense of the person accused.

A good guide for applying penalties by way of the extrajudicial or the administrative penal process in cases covered by the Latin Code would be to use it solely in those cases wherein the proofs actually arising from the preliminary

1 Canon 1434 §1. In addition to all things mentioned in canon 1431 §1, a major excommunication forbids one to receive other sacraments, to administer sacraments and sacramentals, to exercise any offices, ministries and functions, to place acts of governance, which, if they are nonetheless placed, are null by law itself.

§2. One punished with a major excommunication is to be turned away from participating in the Divine Liturgy and in other public celebrations of divine worship.

§3. One punished with a major excommunication is forbidden to make use of privileges previously granted. He cannot validly obtain dignities, offices, ministries, or any other function in the Church or a pension, and he cannot acquire the revenues attached to them. Moreover, he is deprived of active and passive voice.

investigation are evident. Although the one being investigated may spontaneously confess in some way to committing the crime when confronted with such certain proofs, a penal process is still needed; and the administrative penal process would certainly be appropriate in such a case. However, using the judicial process would be a good rule of thumb for cases under the Latin Code because of what we learn from the history of the development of canon 1342 of the *CIC* as well as from a look at the *CCEO*.

Rev. Msgr. Fred C. Easton, JCL

Canons 1355 and 1364

Remission of a Doubtfully-Incurred *Latæ Sententiæ* Excommunication

A man baptised and brought up as a Catholic drifted away from the practice of the faith in early adulthood. Some years later he was brought back to Christianity by protestant evangelicals, and was eventually ordained in a non-Catholic ecclesial community. Now he wishes to be reconciled to the Catholic Church. He has no desire to be a Catholic priest, but does wish to have his status in the Church clarified because he does not wish to cause scandal. Has he committed a delict and incurred a penalty which requires canonical intervention?

Opinion

In the case presented, there are all sorts of questions about which delicts have been committed. Those mentioned in canons 1364 (heresy and schism), 1365 (forbidden *communicatio in sacris*), possibly 1366 (handing over children to be baptised and brought up in a non-Catholic religion), 1371 (teaching condemned doctrines) and 1378–1379 (simulation of sacraments) might all be applicable. Were there a question of declaring or imposing penalties, the competent Ordinary or judge would have to examine the facts and circumstances very carefully to establish whether a delict was committed and whether any of the extenuating or mitigating circumstances of canons 1323–1324 were present.

Given the man's current situation, however, it all seems rather moot. He now repents and seems to be keen to make reparation and to avoid or repair scandal; in other words he has purged his contempt (cf. c. 1347 §2). Thus, if he did in fact incur a *latæ sententiæ* censure, he now has the right to have it remitted (c. 1358 §1). There is little point going to the trouble of establishing whether or not a censure has been incurred if it has to be remitted anyway.

Were it clear that a censure had been incurred, the Ordinary could remit the penalties (c. 1355 §2); indeed, he could not refuse to do so. He can therefore certainly remit them *ad cautelam* if it is not clear whether or not the censure has been incurred: "If it be necessary, by the power granted to me, I absolve you from the bond of excommunication in the name of the Father, and of the Son, and of the Holy Spirit." This remission can be granted personally or through a suitable delegate such as the parish priest (cf. c. 137 §1).

Without arduous enquiry it is difficult to say whether the man committed a delict and incurred a penalty which strictly requires canonical intervention. But even without such enquiry, a simple canonical intervention can nevertheless give certainty that the man is free from censure, bringing both peace to his conscience and clarity for all concerned.

Rev. Benjamin Earl, OP, JCL

CANON 1673

IDENTIFYING THE COMPETENT ECCLESIASTICAL COURT

Can the judicial vicar of the place where the respondent has a domicile or quasi-domicile delegate the moderator of the tribunal chancery to give consent, after having heard the respondent, to the claim of competence of the tribunal of the domicile of the petitioner in a marriage nullity case?

OPINION

In virtue of his office, the judicial vicar enjoys ordinary judicial power of governance for all cases, except those that the diocesan bishop has reserved to himself (c. 1420 §§1-2). This judicial power cannot be validly delegated (c. 135 §3). However, not all of the tasks incumbent on the judicial vicar involve the exercise of judicial power of governance. Rather, like the Chief Justice of the Supreme Court of the United States, the judicial vicar performs a variety of "housekeeping" functions of an administrative or perhaps quasi-administrative character to insure the smooth operation of the tribunal. These tasks include: constituting tribunals by assigning personnel to hear and decide cases submitted to the tribunal (c. 1425 §3), substituting tribunal personnel for cases for most grave reasons (c. 1425 §5), notifying the local ordinary of the place where a marriage was celebrated when an affirmative decision has been rendered and confirmed in a marriage case (c. 1685), and consenting to the claims of competence by tribunals of the domicile of the petitioner or of the place where the majority of proofs are to be gathered (c. 1673, 3°-4°).

In principle, "ordinary executive power of governance can be delegated for a single act or for all cases unless the law expressly provides otherwise" (c. 137 §1). The law raises no barrier to the delegation of administrative responsibilities in the tribunal. In fact, it is clear that the judicial vicar can be delegated to perform a variety of administrative functions reserved by law to the diocesan bishop: appointing judges out of turn in particular cases (c. 1425 §3), committing marriage cases to a single clerical judge (c. 1425 §4), determining when the intervention of the promoter of justice is called for in particular cases (c. 1431 §1), allowing judges from other dioceses to collect proofs in his tribunal's territory (c. 1469 §2), and admitting advocates to function in the tribunal (c. 1483).

If the judicial vicar can be delegated to perform administrative tasks the law assigns explicitly to the diocesan bishop, there seems to be no reason why the moderator of the tribunal chancery cannot be delegated to perform housekeeping tasks the law assigns to the judicial vicar.

The nature of the action of the judicial vicar of the respondent when he consents to the claim of competence by the judicial vicar of the domicile of the petitioner, or of the place where most of the proofs must be gathered, has been badly obscured by misleading language used by practitioners. When canonists speak of "asking" for, "requesting," or "seeking" competence and "granting" or "giving" competence, they suggest that what the judicial vicar is doing is delegating competence or judicial power to the other tribunal's judge or judges. However, as the law and the Apostolic Signatura have made clear, delegation of judicial power by authorities below the level of the Apostolic See is invalid. (c. 135 §3). When marriage cases are submitted to the tribunals of the domicile of the petitioner or to the tribunal in whose territory the majority of proofs must be gathered, it is the law itself that grants these tribunals competence, but on condition that (*dummodo*) the judicial vicar of the respondent consents. The reason for this condition is to assure that the respondent is not unduly hindered from participating or defending his or her interests in the case by the choice of a forum more convenient to the petitioner. Thus, the consent of the judicial vicar of the respondent is analogous to the consenting vote of the diocesan finance council to the bishop's proposal to perform an act of extraordinary administration (c. 1277). The consent authorizes the diocesan bishop to move ahead with the action he had proposed, but it does not delegate him the authority to perform the act. In the same way, the judicial vicar of the respondent, after hearing the respondent, can opt to consent or not to the other tribunal's assertion of competence. He does not, however, give that other tribunal anything it does not already have except a sort of *nihil obstat* allowing it to exercise the judicial power granted it, albeit conditionally, by the law. As a result, the consent by the judicial vicar of the respondent is not really an act of governance at all; and the authority to grant this consent can be delegated to some other person such as the moderator of the tribunal chancery.

Rev. John P. Beal, JCD

CANON 1682 AND *DIGNITAS CONNUBII*, ART. 265 §1 AND 291 §2

WHETHER THE SUBSTANTIAL CONFORMITY OF DECISIONS CAN BE DECLARED IN A DECREE OF CONFIRMATION OF AN AFFIRMATIVE SENTENCE IN CAUSES OF THE NULLITY OF MARRIAGE

At our appellate tribunal, we often need to decide whether or not to confirm by decree an affirmative sentence of the first instance tribunal, when we are convinced that an inappropriate ground was used by the lower tribunal, while we are also convinced that the marriage is null on a related ground. Can we simply confirm the affirmative sentence on the unnamed ground for the sake of the parties?

OPINION

When the superior judges are required to decide whether to confirm an affirmative sentence immediately or to admit it to an ordinary examination, they must answer the question as to whether the nullity of the marriage is proven with respect to the doubt(s) to which an affirmative response was given in the same sentence. They are obliged to decide to confirm the conclusion (*pars dispositiva)* of the affirmative decision *as it is*, not as they think *it should be*; in other words, they must determine whether they are morally certain that the nullity of the marriage is proven on the same ground(s) decided affirmatively in the sentence.[1] Therefore, as a rule, art. 291 §2 of the Instruction *Dignitas connubii* does not apply to the decree of confirmation in the *processus brevior*.

1 "Once a sentence in the first degree of jurisdiction has been issued in favour of the nullity of a marriage, the appellate tribunal can only confirm that decision immediately by its decree in relation to the ground of nullity for which there is an affirmative sentence in the first degree. Otherwise, the cause in the appellate degree must be admitted to an ordinary examination, and the decision in favour of the nullity of the marriage cannot be issued by means of a decree (cf. c. 1682 §2). An affirmative decision, therefore, cannot be issued by means of a decree if it concerns a ground of nullity for which the appellate tribunal is issuing the first decision."

Supreme Tribunal of the Apostolic Signatura, Response, October 30, 1997, prot. no. 26882/96 VT, no. 1, in *Ministerium Iustitiæ. Jurisprudence of the Supreme Tribunal of the Apostolic Signatura. Official Latin with English Translation*, ed. William L. Daniel, Gratianus Series, (Montréal, Wilson & Lafleur Ltée, 2011) 739.

See also, e.g., Tribunal of the Roman Rota, Decree *c.* Bruno, November 25, 1994, no. 6, in *RRT Decreta*, 12 (1994) 189; Decree *c.* Pompedda, October 24, 1997, no. 3, in *RRT Decreta*, 15 (1997) 236.

This is born out especially in the requirement of the motivation of the decree of confirmation—an act which has the same character as a definitive sentence (*ad instar sententiæ definitivæ*). The decree of confirmation cannot be a mere template containing little or nothing specific to the cause at hand; it must articulate at least briefly the juridical principles (*in iure*) and arguments (*in facto*) that motivate the superior judges to confirm the sentence, even if they are substantially the same as those in the affirmative sentence, and give a just response to any observations of the second instance defender of the bond and the parties. When confirming an affirmative sentence, the superior judges underscore the correspondence of the affirmative sentence to the proven facts and its due response to the formula of the doubt. It would be absurd for the decree of confirmation to contain a rationale that undermines the affirmative sentence, by expressing doubt about the ground decided affirmatively and arguing in favor of a doubt not previously raised. And of course it would be *contra veritatem* in such a case for the judges simply to issue a decree of confirmation on an "unnamed ground."

There may be possible exceptions, such as when the argumentation and the ground of nullity on which the affirmative sentence is based is inclusive of some other ground of nullity included subordinately in the first instance formulation of the doubt. For example, the formulation of the doubt proposes the nullity of the marriage principally on the basis of total simulation (i.e., exclusion of marriage itself) by the respondent and subordinately on the basis of his or her partial simulation *contra bonum sacramenti*, and the sentence declares the nullity of consent based only on the respondent's total simulation (which would exclude all the *bona* of marriage), on the basis of proven facts which concern in particular the *bonum sacramenti.* If the appellate college of judges is morally certain only of the respondent's exclusion of the *bonum sacramenti*, it is possible (by a certain analogy with *DC*, art. 265 §6) that the sentence could be legitimately confirmed by a decree, which would need to explain very clearly how the exclusion of the *bonum sacramenti* has been demonstrated at least implicitly in the argumentation of the sentence and is implicitly included in its conclusion.

Such an exception is clearly not possible in other cases, for instance, when the affirmative sentence declares the nullity of the marriage by reason of the petitioner's incapacity due to a grave defect of discretion of judgment, while the superior judges think, on the other hand, that the petitioner's total simulation is the more appropriate ground. A decree of confirmation that demonstrates that the party deliberately and willfully rejected marriage itself would undermine the conclusion of the affirmative sentence that he was incapable of directing his will toward marriage due to a psychological anomaly. Such a "decree of confirmation" would in fact at least implicitly declare that the affirmative decision pertaining to the alleged incapacity could not be confirmed, and thus it would lack the essential elements constitutive of a decree of confirmation.

To continue using this example, in presuming to declare the nullity of the marriage due to total simulation in the decree of confirmation, the superior judge's act is in fact not only invalid but even non-existent in many respects:

1. If the appellate tribunal is not also a first instance tribunal, its decree of confirmation is irremediably null due to its absolute incompetence (c. 1620 1°), since it in effect is deciding a new ground as if in first instance (c. 1683).
2. The judges cannot presume to introduce a new ground purely on their own initiative and unbeknownst to the parties, since this would entail the judicial resolution of a question never introduced by a judicial petition (c. 1620 4°). *Nemo iudex sine actore.*
3. The parties' right of defense would be denied by such an act, since they would never have had an opportunity to present any responses, evidence, or arguments pertaining to the alleged total simulation. The second instance defender of the bond's right of defense would likewise be denied if the judges made this innovation after he or she presented his or her *votum prævium* (c. 1620 7°).
4. And the decree of confirmation would be inexistent since it would not even partially decide the controversy (c. 1620 8°). The controversy is whether or not the sentence declaring the petitioner's incapacity is to be confirmed, that is, whether the petitioner's incapacity is proven. Should the decree of confirmation declare the petitioner's total simulation, the judges would entirely neglect the question entrusted to their judicial ministry.

Would it be legitimate for the decree of confirmation to assent to the arguments in favor of the incapacity of the petitioner (with which they in fact disagree), while in fact the judges themselves sustain moral certitude in their minds only about his or her total simulation? Absolutely not: this approach would be a grave violation of the integrity so essential to the judicial office and betray an erroneous understanding of moral certitude, which is objective and publicly demonstrable in the sentence or decree. This would be no service to the parties but a disingenuous action betraying the tribunal's divorcist mentality (or its orientation to "help" petitioners by ratifying in the Church the civil dissolution of the marriage contract).

What can the superior judges do instead of issuing such a defective or dishonest decree of confirmation? In the first place, if they are not morally certain of the nullity of marriage as demonstrated by the affirmative sentence, they must admit the cause to an ordinary examination.[2] Then, in perceiving that the proven facts suggest a ground not yet established as a term of the controversy, on the occasion of the admission of the cause to an ordinary examination when the judge calls the parties to trial by the citation, the judge may declare his or her intention to include the new, more appropriate ground in the formula of the doubt, giving the parties fifteen useful days to reply.[3] The formula of the doubt containing the new ground and the original ground(s) would also include this doubt: "If affirmative on the new ground, whether the substantial conformity of the first and second instance sentences is established in the case." The appellate trial then continues as normal, with supplementary instruction if necessary, the publication of the acts, and the conclusion and discussion of the cause. Finally, if the college of judges is morally certain that the nullity of marriage on the new ground is established on the basis of the same proven facts as those on which the first instance affirmative sentence is based, the second instance sentence declares the nullity of the marriage on the new ground and the substantial conformity of itself with the first instance affirmative sentence (*DC*, art. 291 §2).

Mr. William L. Daniel, JCL

2 "In this case, having observed all that is necessary, the appellate tribunal can adjudicate the matter only by means of the ordinary process" (Supreme Tribunal of the Apostolic Signatura, Response, October 30, 1997, *cit.* [*vide supra* note 1], no. 1, p. 739).

3 Cf. cc. 1452 §1; 1677 §2; *DC*, art. 127 §2. The judge should not force this ground into the trial; if the spouses or the defender of the bond present reasonable objections, the judge should remain detached from the matter and refrain from adding the ground.

Contributors

Rev. Jobe J. Abbass, OFM Conv., JCD, is a Professor of Canon Law at Saint Paul University, Ottawa, Ontario, Canada.

Rev. John P. Beal, JCD, is a Professor of Canon Law at the Catholic University of America, Washington, DC.

Rev. Brendan P. Daly, JCD, is Principal of Good Shepherd College in Auckland, New Zealand and Associate Judicial Vicar in the Regional Tribunal of New Zealand.

Mr. William L. Daniel, JCL, is Vice-Chancellor and Judge in the Diocese of Winona, Minnesota.

Rev. Benjamin Earl, OP, JCL is a priest of St. Cuthbert's Parish in Durham, England, and Catholic Chaplain to Durham University in England.

Rev. Msgr. Fred C. Easton, JCL, is the Adjutant Judicial Vicar for the Diocese of Indianapolis, Indiana.

Dr. Chad J. Glendinning, JCD, is an Assistant Professor of Canon Law at Saint Paul University, Ottawa, Ontario, Canada.

Dr. John M. Huels, JCD, is a Professor of Canon Law at Saint Paul University, Ottawa, Ontario, Canada.

Rev. Edwin N. Omorogbe, JCD, is the Assistant Pastor at Our Lady of Fatima Parish in Ottawa, Ontario, Canada.

Mr. Matthew Orzolek, JCL, is a full-time doctoral student at the Catholic University of America in Washington, DC.

Rev. Msgr. John A. Renken, STD, JCD, is a Professor of Canon Law at Saint Paul University, Ottawa, Ontario, Canada.

Rev. Msgr. Michael A. Souckar, JCD, is the Adjutant Judicial Vicar for the Archdiocese of Miami and the Pastor at St. Andrew Catholic Church in Coral Springs, Florida.

Ms. Amy Strickland, JCL, is a canon lawyer residing in the Archdiocese of Washington, DC.